PLANETARIA

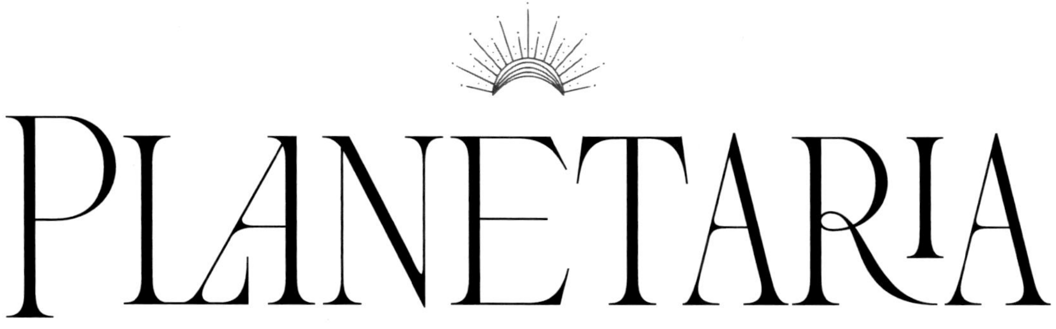

VISUAL POETRY

MONICA ONG

Foreword by John Yau

PROXIMA VERA
Trumbull, Connecticut

Published by Proxima Vera
Trumbull, Connecticut 06611
www.proximavera.com

Book and cover design by Monica Ong
This book was composed in Adobe Caslon Pro and Adorn Serif
Display title typeface set in Asther © Ivan Rosenberg www.youworkforthem.com
Cover background texture The Star Atlas © Blixa 6 Studios www.youworkforthem.com

Library of Congress Control Number: 2024921974
ISBN 979-8-218-51006-0

The main stumbling block in the way of any progress is and always has been unimpeachable tradition.

—CHIEN-SHIUNG WU

TABLE OF CONTENTS

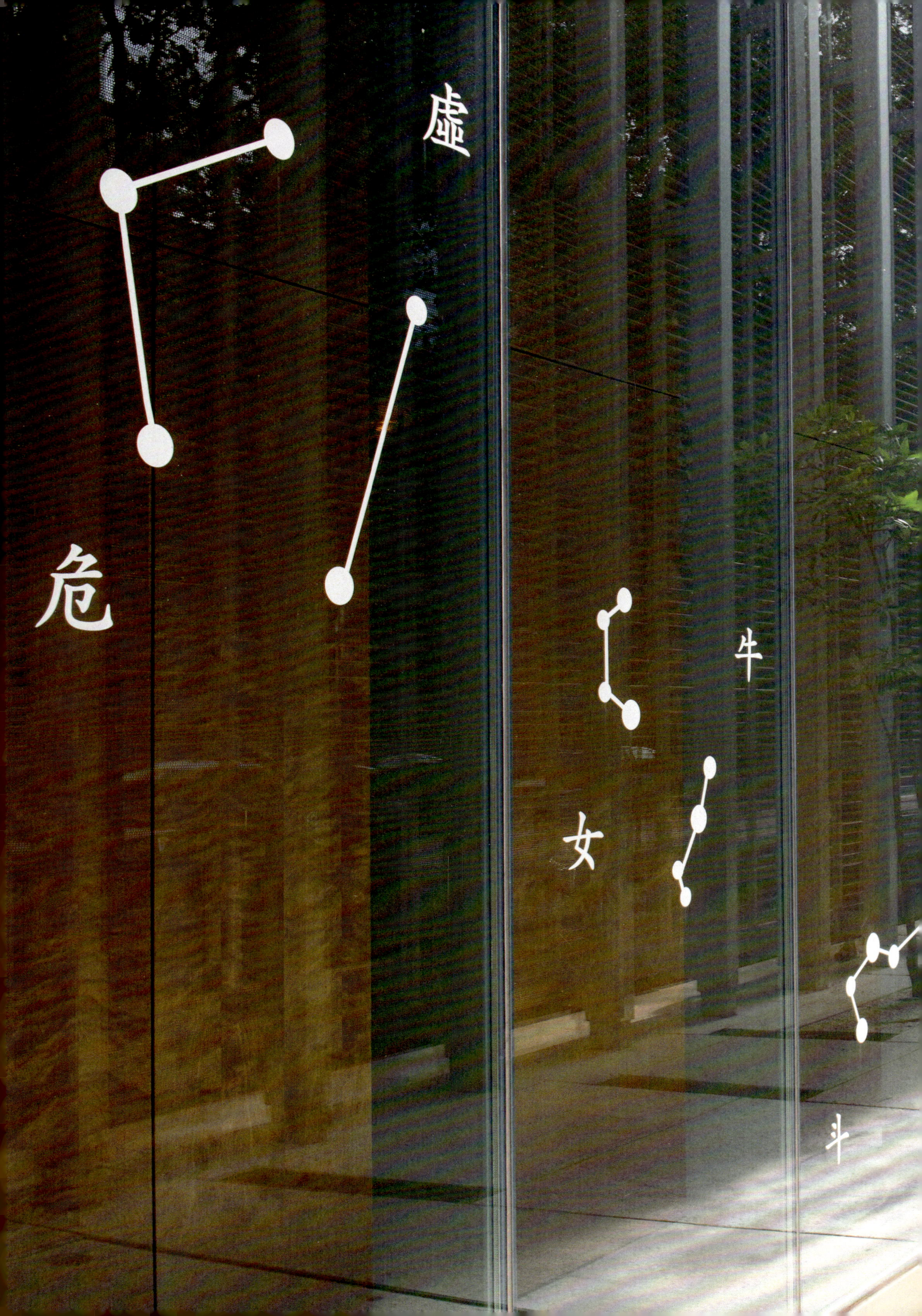
虛
危
牛
女
斗

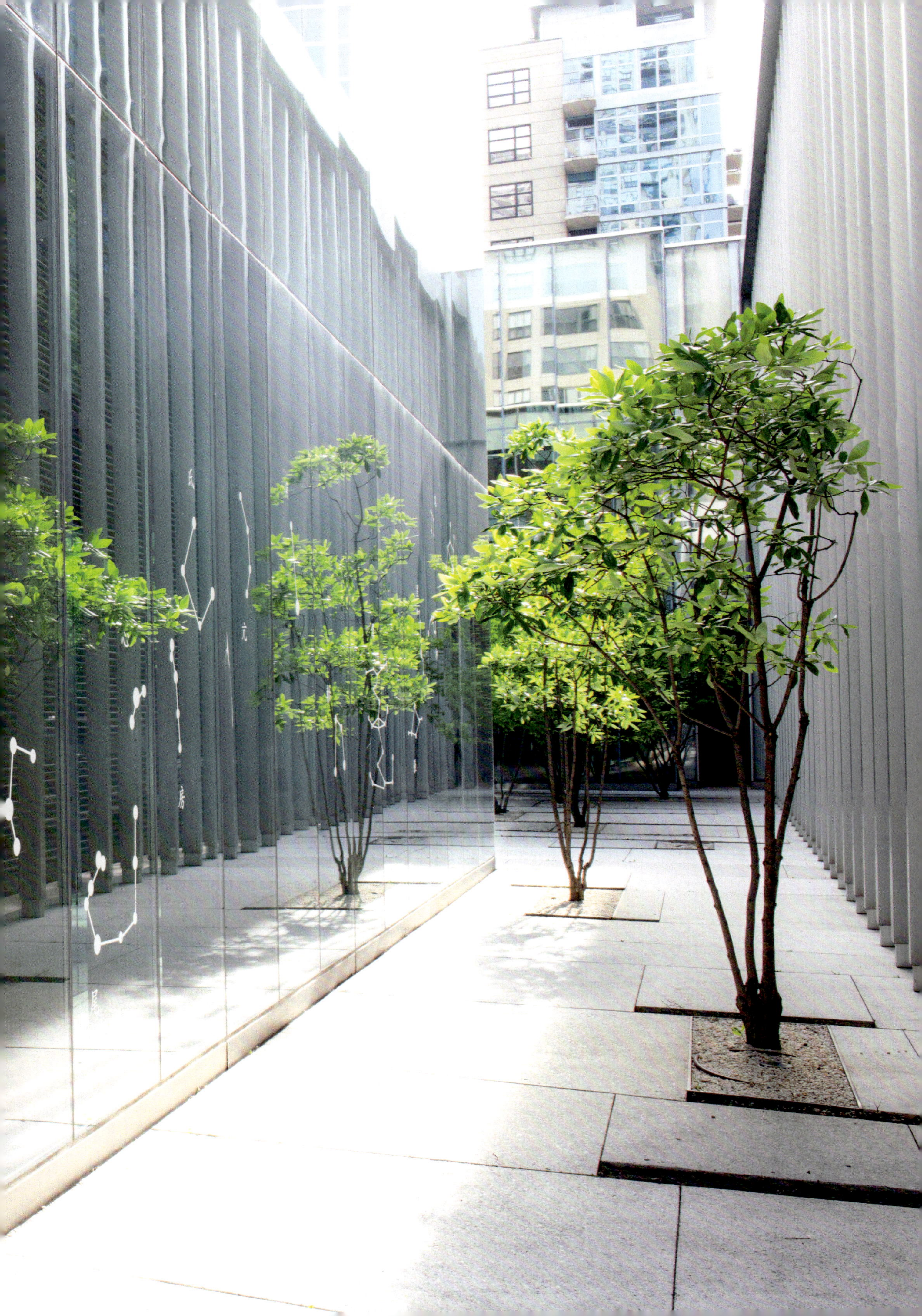

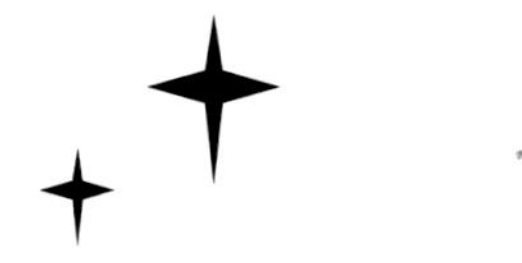

Foreword

John Yau

At the beginning of her marvelous book, *Planetaria,* Monica Ong declares her intention with an epigram taken from Chien-Shiung Wu, a Chinese-American particle and experimental physicist, who was known as the 'Queen of Nuclear Research':

> *The main stumbling block in the way of any progress is and always has been unimpeachable tradition.*

Instead of aligning her writing with an established, avant-garde agenda, Ong has defined a fresh trajectory that arises out of living in the diaspora while being aware that we inhabit an expanding universe. By incorporating family photographs, Chinese star charts, astronomy texts, scientific diagrams, unwritten and neglected histories and biographies, and symbolic language, she is able to synthesize aspects of the microcosmic and macrocosmic into something original and disruptive.

Ong's visual poems replete with charged language expose the obstacles shaping an individual's life. Motivated by a propelling desire to dissolve the constraints of literary tradition, gender bias, family history, and cultural beliefs, she has intervened in classical Chinese texts and written shaped poems in praise of women scientists, always making something new.

Her precise breaches mark a break with the familiar immigrant narratives of families living in the diaspora, unable to free themselves from tradition. Knowing that tradition can stifle the individual's growth, Ong's constantly expanding practice is in tune with science's understanding of the universe's changing conditions, as well as the advice we get from astrologers and the I-Ching. Scientifically minded, which is to say a pursuer of truths, Ong's work is not about superstition, but the long shadows such beliefs cast across time. Discovering the different ways culture has defined the space between the truth-seeking individual and the indifferent universe, she re-envisions that gap.

In 1964, Jasper Johns wrote this in a notebook: "Take an object / Do something to it / Do something else to it. [Repeat.]" Ong is a poet who has heeded Johns' advice. She has combined a Chinese star chart with a family photograph, as well as added words to the descriptions of Chinese asterisms (or constellations). Ong's work embodies the fresh outlook that comes by exposing and breaking apart history. Her culminations are unlike anything else being done in poetry today.

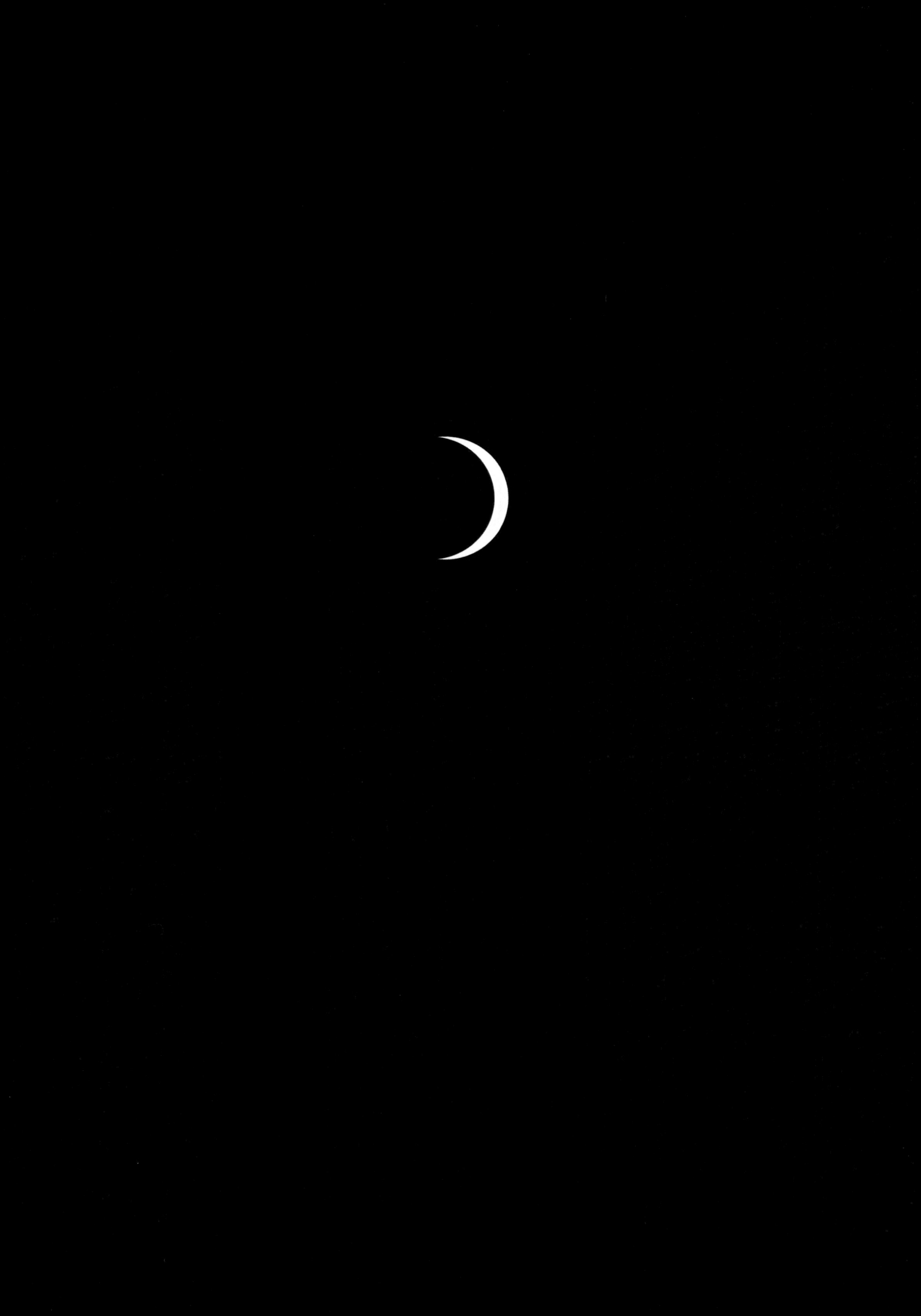

LAVENDER INSOMNIA

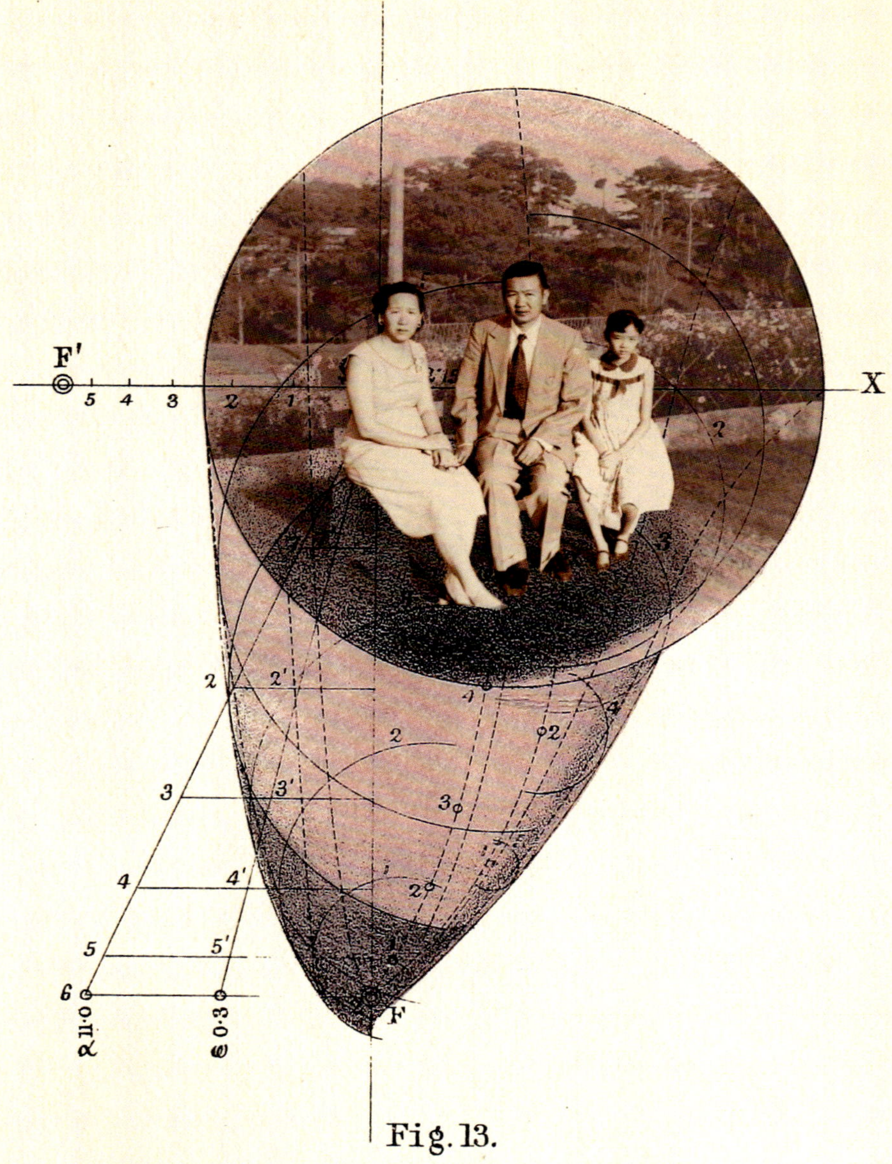

Fig. 13.

Lavender insomnia is my damp hair crying on the pillow. Dirty silverware in the graveyard kitchen buried beneath a long gloom. The crater's quality of silence after collapse that echoes aunt Juanita's sadness, her moon memory a whispered veil hanging from the window over the stairs. Jealous of winter vetiver and basil's rise in spring, lavender insomnia conspires with the body to step back off the edge of a cliff. Its purpled hands submerge the breath beneath an overturned boat. Grinds teeth like a dull blade biding its time. The tall numbers of every hour and every minute burn into the blackened doors shut tight in my eyes that long for a glimpse of the dreaming meadow. Violet and vine, she slips her lady fingers into the mind behind the blue firs. Stirs a hive of bees. The hundred eyes of my ancestors—still waiting for justice—gaze back at me.

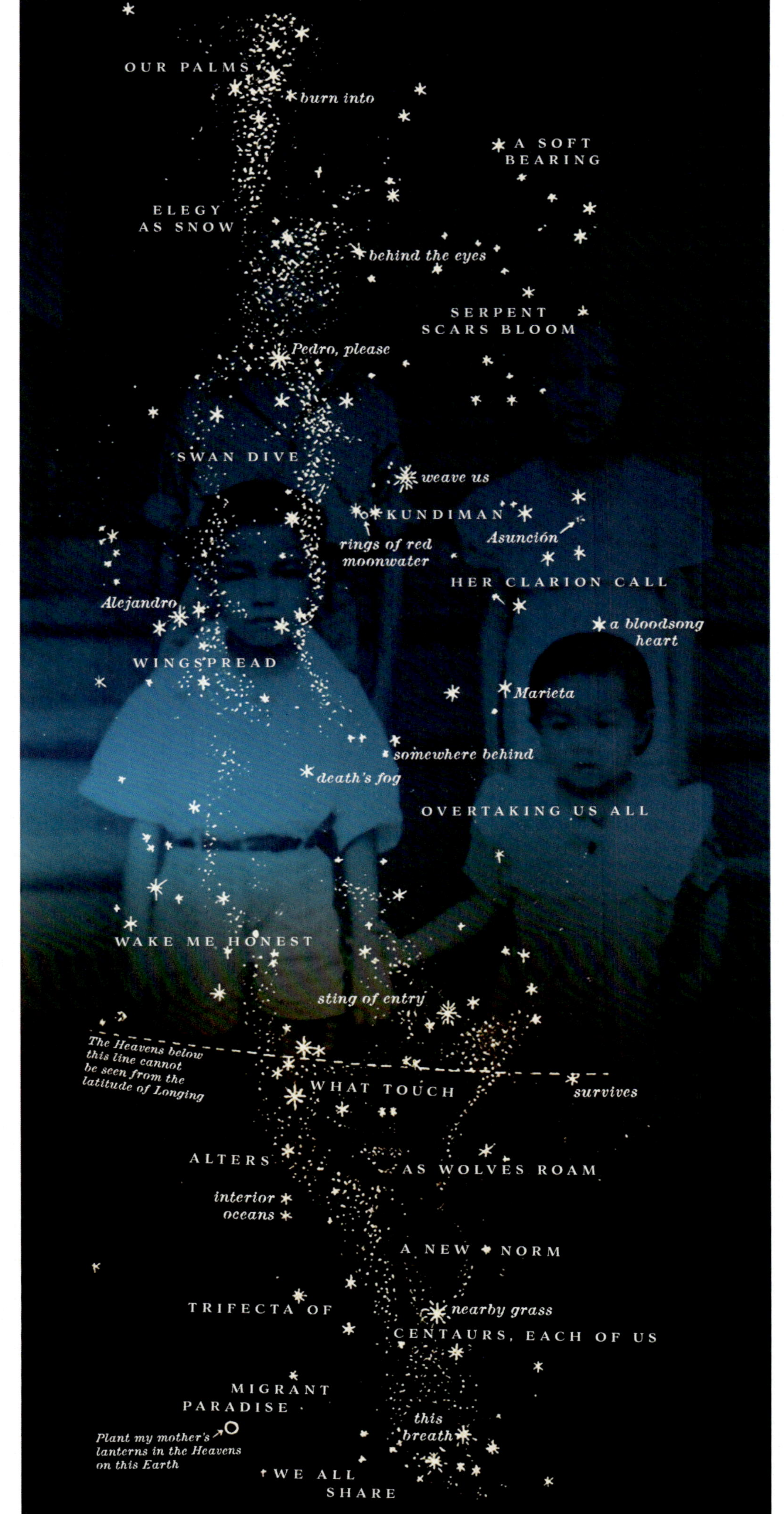
OUR PALMS
burn into
A SOFT
BEARING
ELEGY
AS SNOW
behind the eyes
SERPENT
SCARS BLOOM
Pedro, please
SWAN DIVE
weave us
KUNDIMAN
rings of red
moonwater
Asunción
HER CLARION CALL
Alejandro
a bloodsong
heart
WINGSPREAD
Marieta
somewhere behind
death's fog
OVERTAKING US ALL
WAKE ME HONEST
sting of entry
The Heavens below
this line cannot
be seen from the
latitude of Longing
WHAT TOUCH
survives
ALTERS
AS WOLVES ROAM
interior
oceans
A NEW NORM
TRIFECTA OF
nearby grass
CENTAURS, EACH OF US
MIGRANT
PARADISE
this
breath
Plant my mother's
lanterns in the Heavens
on this Earth
WE ALL
SHARE

THE WAY OF MILK

Our palms
        burn into   a soft bearing

Elegy as snow
            behind the eyes
                        serpent scars bloom

        Pedro, please
swan dive
            weave us
        Kundiman
    rings of red moonwater   Asunción
                    her clarion call
                            a bloodsong heart

Alejandro
    wingspread   Marieta

                somewhere behind
            death's fog
                    overtaking us all

Wake me honest
            sting of entry

The Heavens below
this line cannot
be seen from the
latitude of Longing

            What touch   survives
alters
interior   as wolves roam
oceans   a new norm

trifecta of   nearby grass
                Centaurs, each of us

    migrant
  paradise

Plant my mother's
lanterns in the Heavens
on this Earth
                this breath
        we all
            share

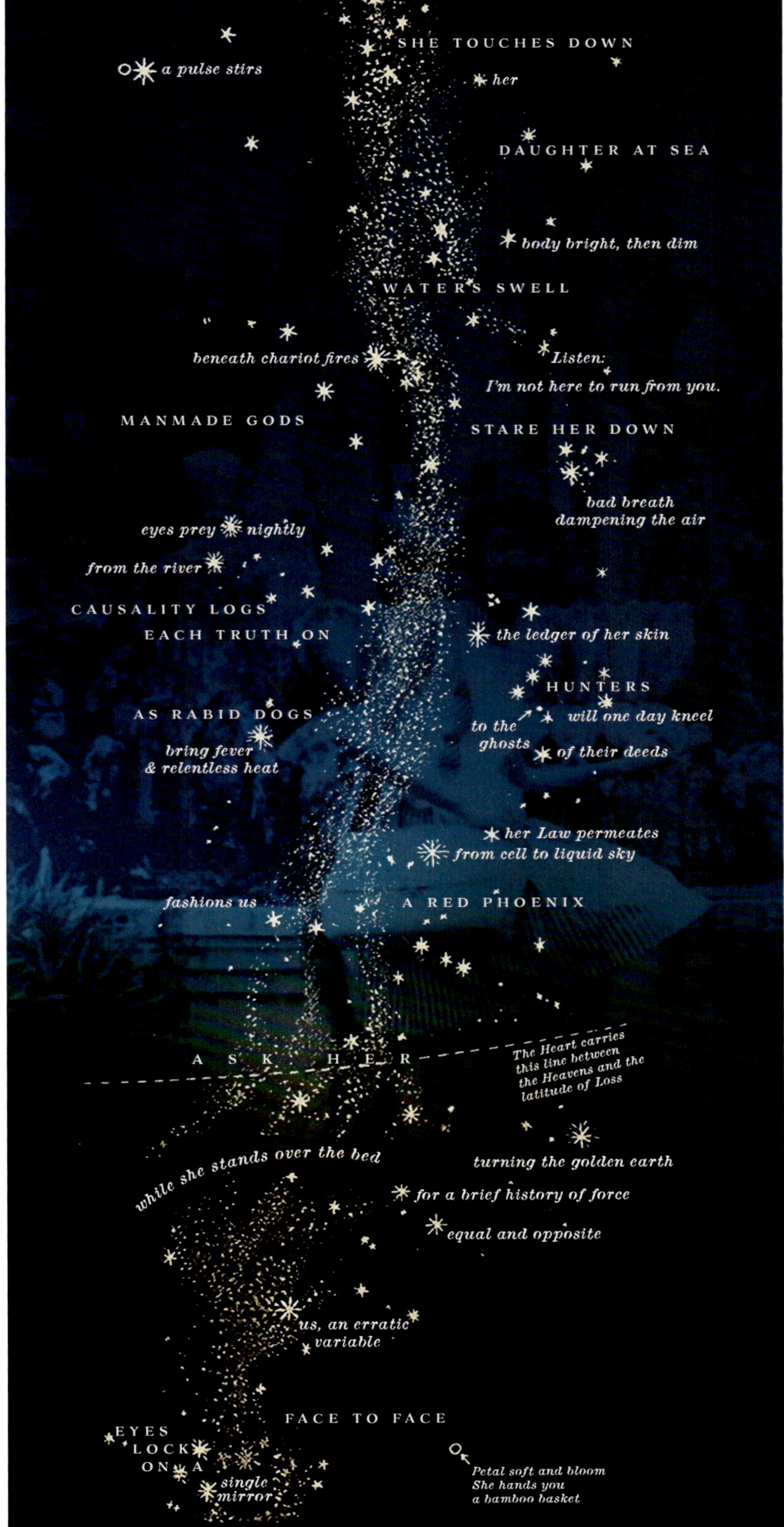
SHE TOUCHES DOWN
a pulse stirs
her
DAUGHTER AT SEA
body bright, then dim
WATERS SWELL
beneath chariot fires
Listen:
I'm not here to run from you.
MANMADE GODS
STARE HER DOWN
bad breath
dampening the air
eyes prey nightly
from the river
CAUSALITY LOGS
EACH TRUTH ON
the ledger of her skin
HUNTERS
AS RABID DOGS
will one day kneel
to the
ghosts
of their deeds
bring fever
& relentless heat
her Law permeates
from cell to liquid sky
fashions us
A RED PHOENIX
ASK HER
The Heart carries
this line between
the Heavens and the
latitude of Loss
while she stands over the bed
turning the golden earth
for a brief history of force
equal and opposite
us, an erratic
variable
FACE TO FACE
EYES
LOCK
ON A
single
mirror
Petal soft and bloom
She hands you
a bamboo basket

THE WAY OF KARMA

She touches down
a pulse stirs her
daughter at sea

body bright, then dim
Waters swell

beneath chariot fires Listen:
I'm not here to run from you

Manmade gods stare her down

bad breath
dampening the air

eyes prey nightly
from the river

Causality logs
each truth on the ledger of her skin

Hunters
as rabid dogs will one day kneel
to the ghosts
of their deeds

bring fever
and relentless heat

her Law permeates
from cell to liquid sky

fashions us a Red Phoenix

Ask Her The heart carries
this line between
the Heavens and the
latitude of Loss

while she stands over the bed

turning the golden earth
for a brief history of force
equal and opposite

us, an erratic
variable

Face to face

Petal soft and bloom
She hands you
a bamboo basket

Eyes lock
on a

single mirror

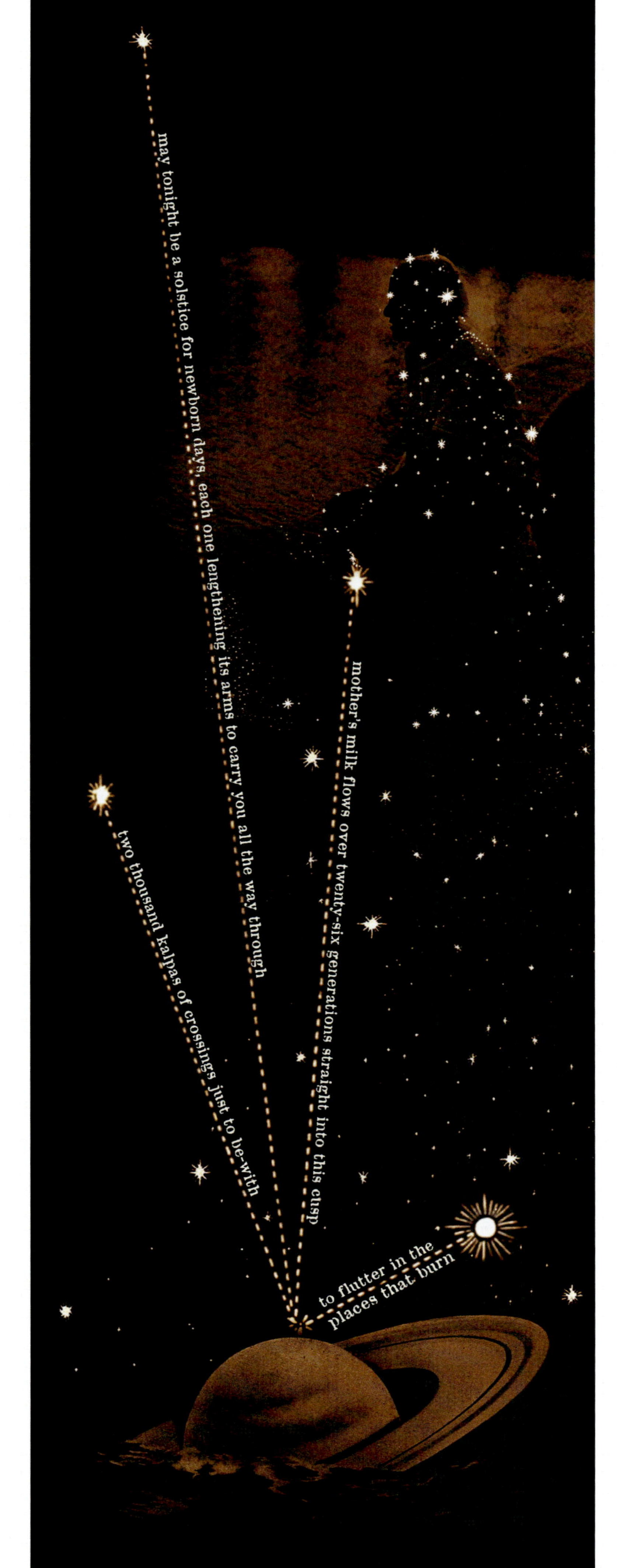
may tonight be a solstice for newborn days, each one lengthening its arms to carry you all the way through
mother's milk flows over twenty-six generations straight into this cusp
two thousand kalpas of crossings just to be-with
to flutter in the places that burn

SOLSTICE BLESSING

may tonight be a solstice
for newborn days,
each one lengthening its arms
to carry you all the way
through

mother's milk
flows over twenty-six
generations
straight into
this cusp

two thousand
kalpas
of crossings
just to
be-with

to flutter in the
places that
burn

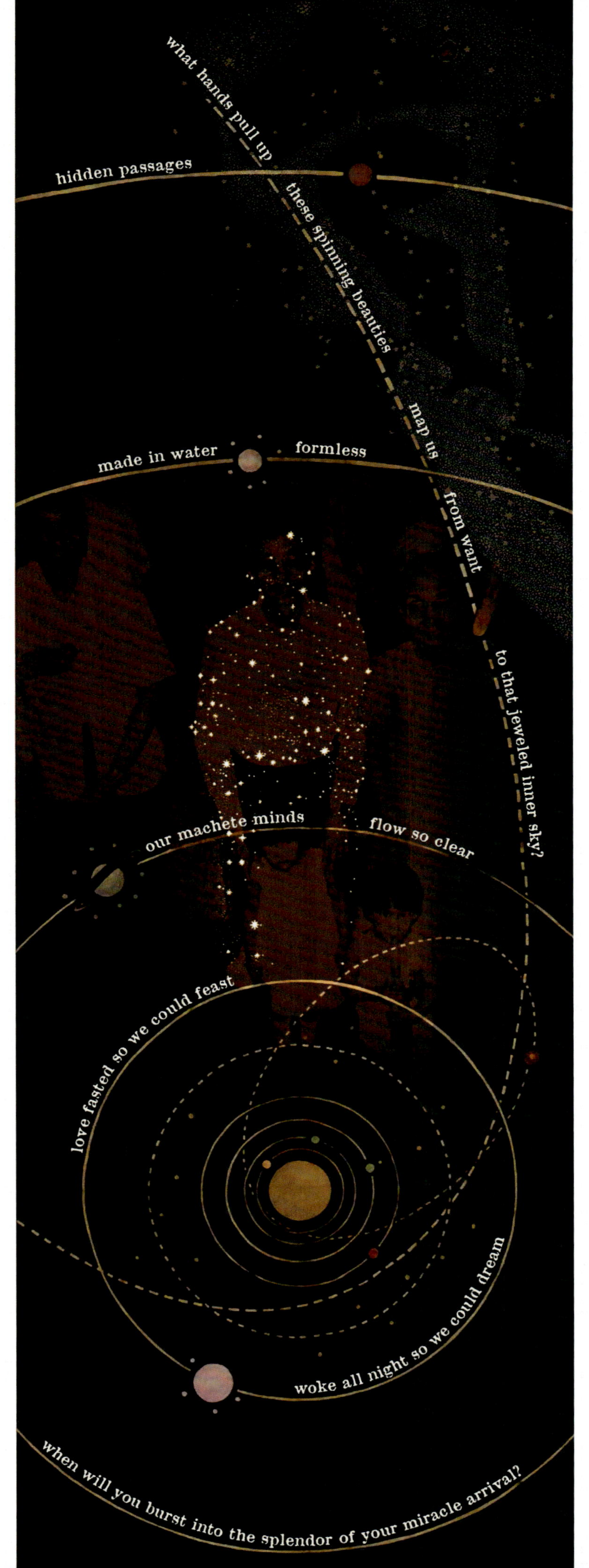
what hands pull up
hidden passages
these spinning beauties
map us
made in water
formless
from want
to that jeweled inner sky?
our machete minds
flow so clear
love fasted so we could feast
woke all night so we could dream
when will you burst into the splendor of your miracle arrival?

DIASPORA NOVA

what hands pull up
these spinning beauties
map us
from want
to that jeweled inner sky?

hidden passages
made in water
formless
our machete minds
flow so clear

love fasted so we could feast
woke all night so we could dream
when will you burst
into the splendor
of your miracle arrival?

PURPLE FORBIDDEN ENCLOSURE

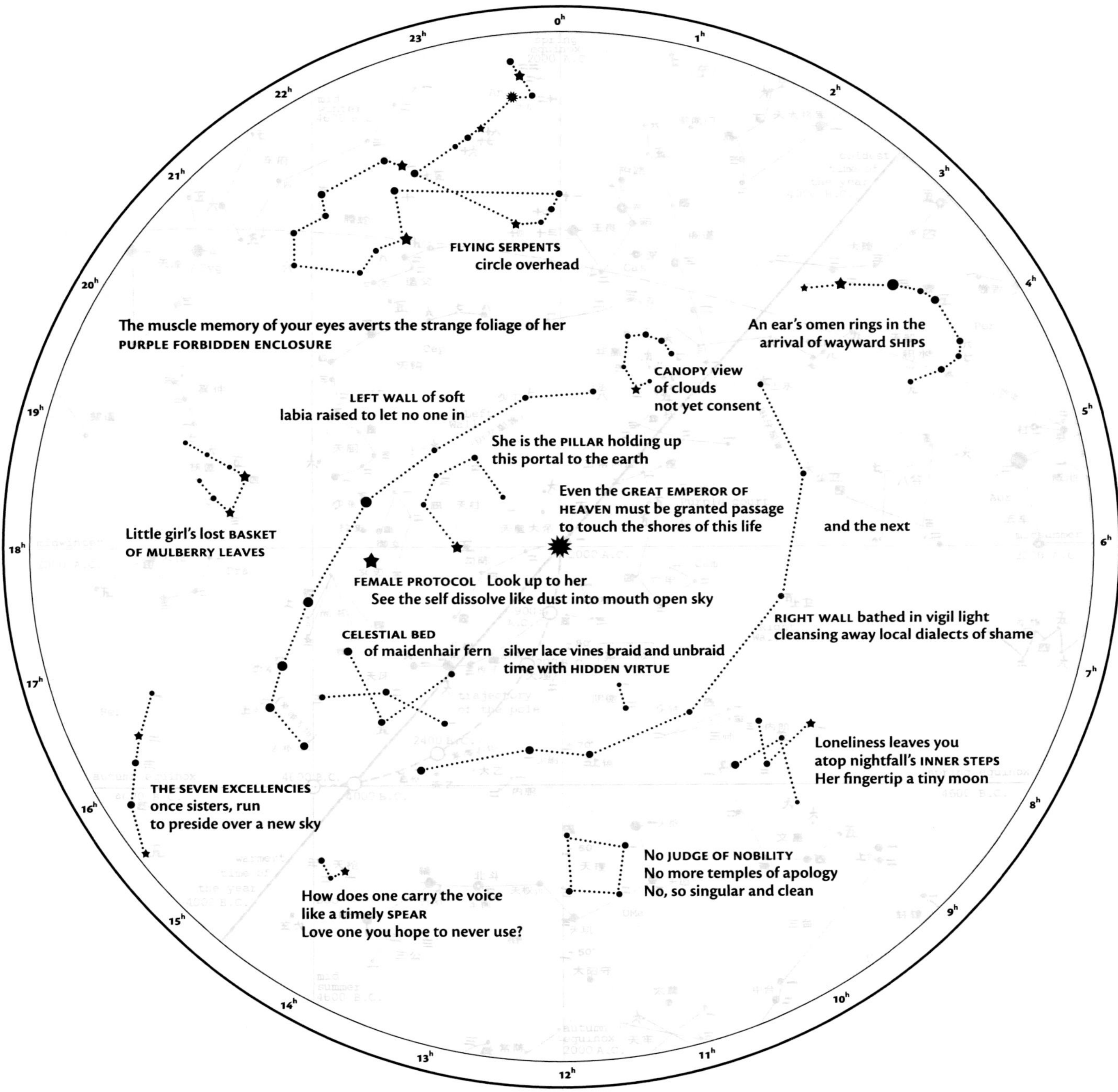

Upper sector of the Northern hemisphere, +40° to +90° declination with selected constellations both inside and outside the walls of the Purple Forbidden Enclosure (紫微垣). Positioned on a celestial north pole, this central court outranks all other courts, its rule of power spread out like a mother's worry from wall to wall, sky to sky.

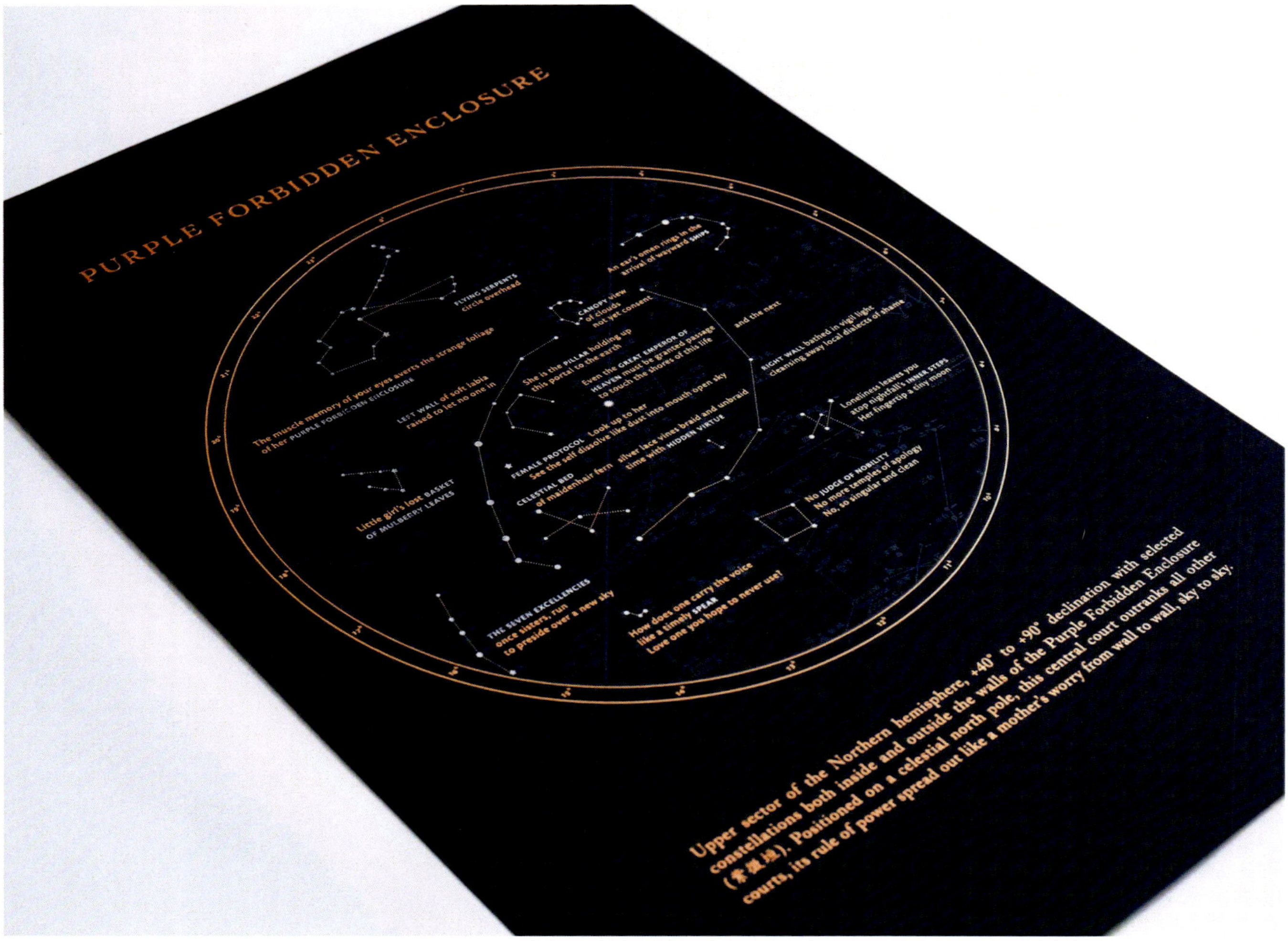

PURPLE FORBIDDEN ENCLOSURE
Upper sector of the Northern hemisphere, +40° to +90° declination with selected constellations both inside and outside the walls of the Purple Forbidden Enclosure (紫微垣). Positioned on a celestial north pole, this central court outranks all other courts, its rule of power spread out like a mother's worry from wall to wall, sky to sky.

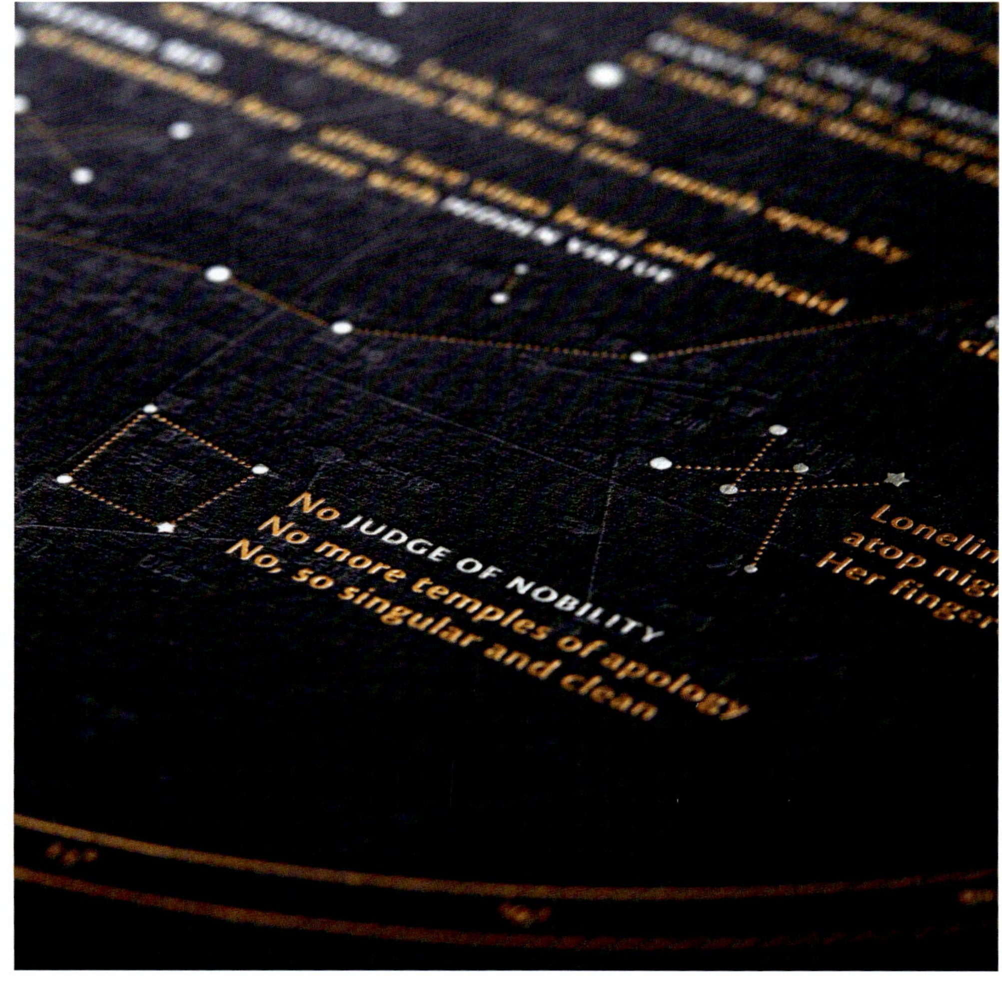
No JUDGE OF NOBILITY
No more temples of apology
No, so singular and clean

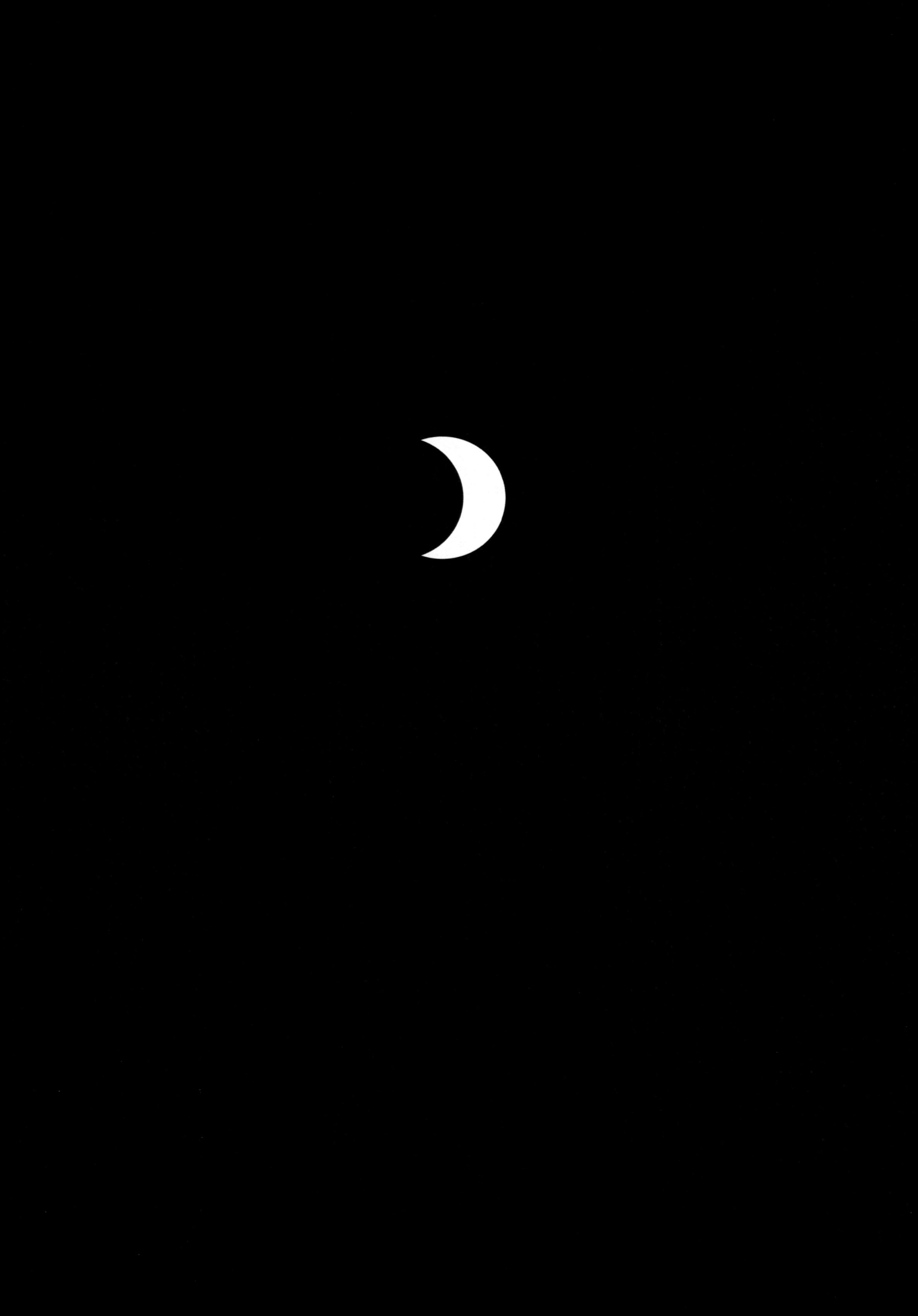

AMBER INSOMNIA

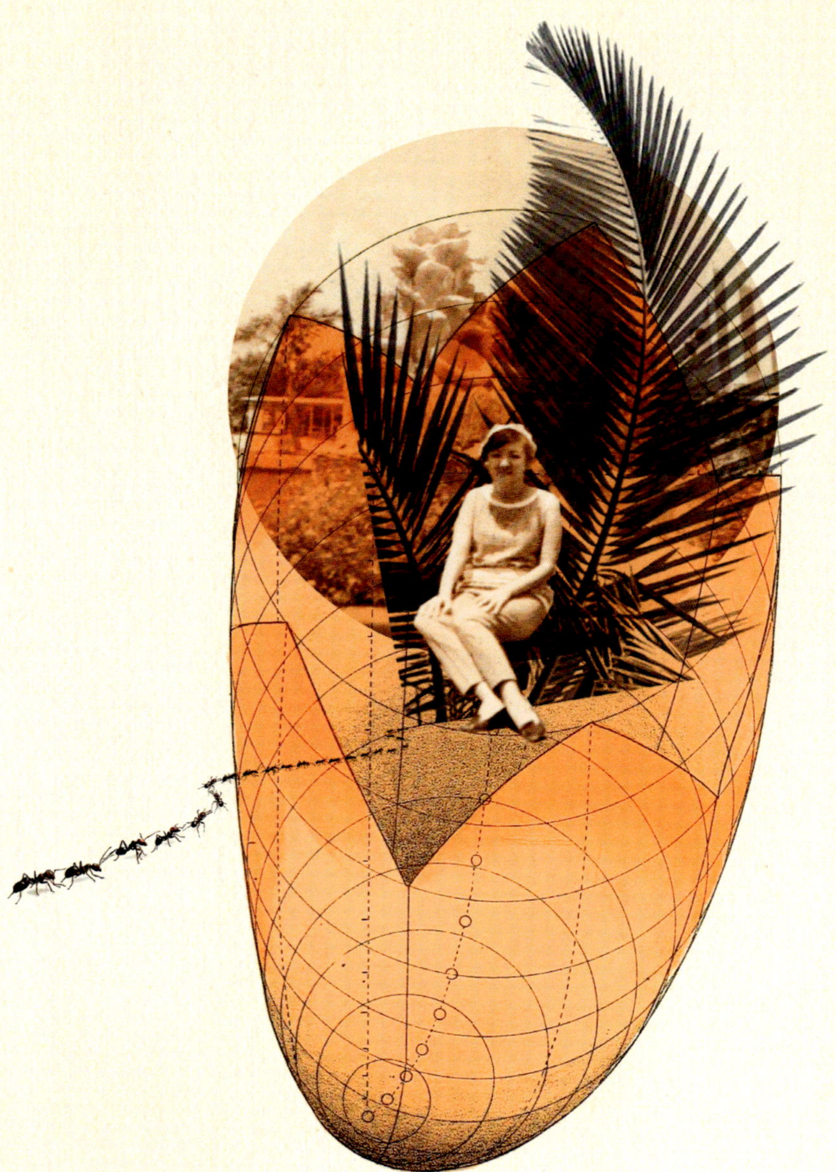

Fig. 12.

Amber insomnia is loneliness hatching an egg in the dark. Each crack glistening, the itch of a wound still open. The constant waking in the skin's red crawl of ants. It is the saffron lining of grandmother's suitcase bursting with plastic packets of thinly sliced mangoes. Sugar and sulfur dust on leathery tongues, a scattered archipelago of sun-dried memories, all of them mistakes (mine) eating away at sleep. What one does and what one wants to do, separated by the sap of a golden hour. The kitchen light hollows out the belly of night, its din curled in the singed husk of a mother caving in. No dream, no slumber. Just an oblong table anchored by a bowl of cold cereal and tremor of tears eating away the deep. Unclosed eyes searching—always—behind the glass. Tonight is a nest deserted or at least the fear of one. Perhaps arrival is not a question of where but when. How opposite trains pausing at the same platform in the same moment look up. Wait. Doors wide open.

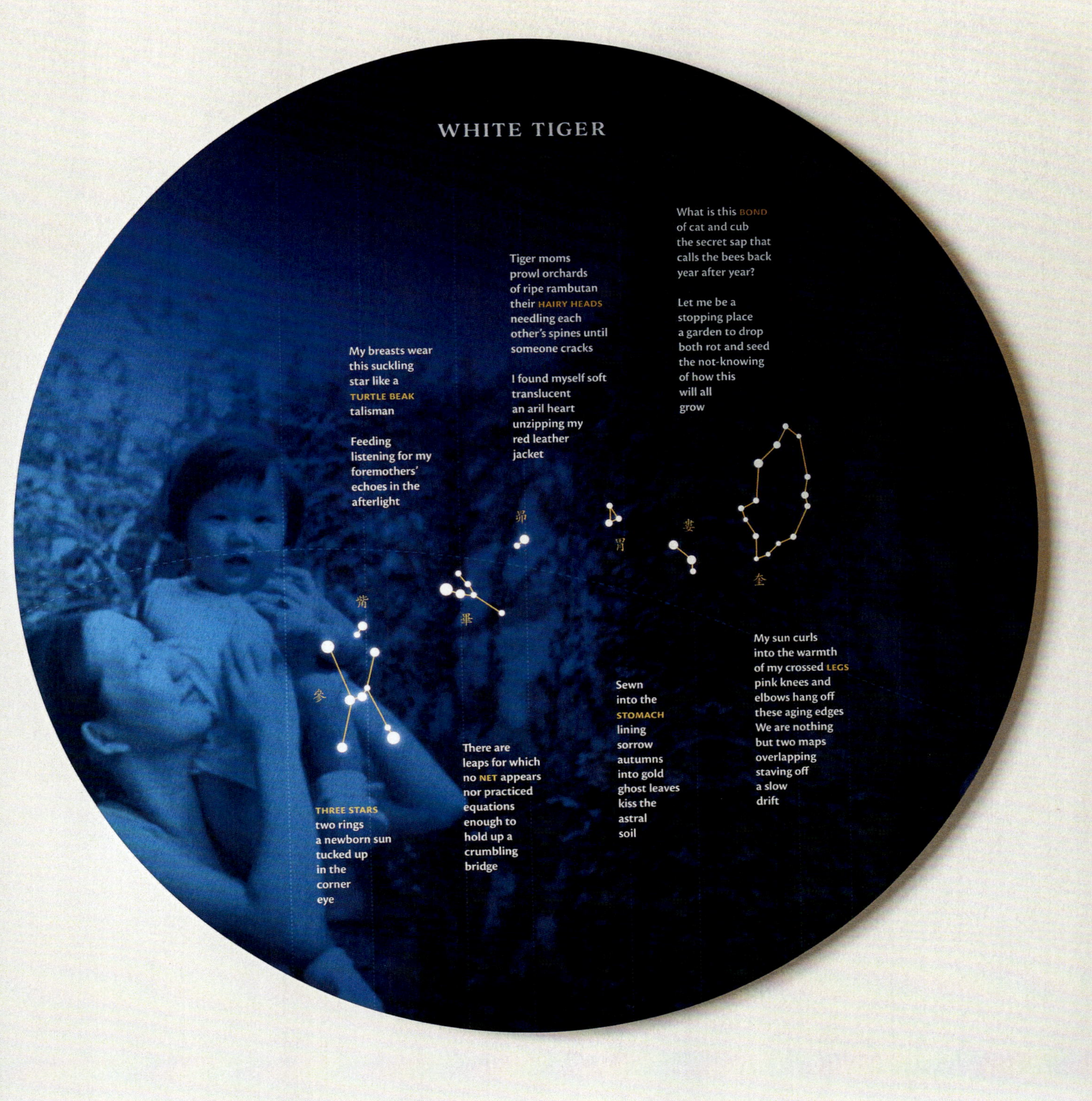

The White Tiger of the western sky rules over seven mansions: Three Stars, Turtle Beak, Net, Hairy Head, Stomach, Bond, and Legs. Associated with the season of autumn and the element of metal, her snowy fur allows her to blend in with her surroundings.

WHITE TIGER

My breasts wear
this suckling
star like a
TURTLE BEAK
talisman

Feeding
listening for my
foremothers'
echoes in the
afterlight

Tiger moms
prowl orchards
of ripe rambutan
their HAIRY HEADS
needling each
other's spines until
someone cracks

I found myself soft
translucent
an aril heart
unzipping my
red leather
jacket

What is this BOND
of cat and cub
the secret sap that
calls the bees back
year after year?

Let me be a
stopping place
a garden to drop
both rot and seed
the not-knowing
of how this
will all
grow

昴

胃

婁

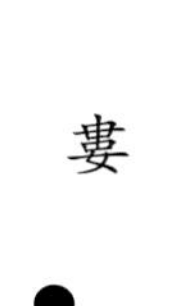

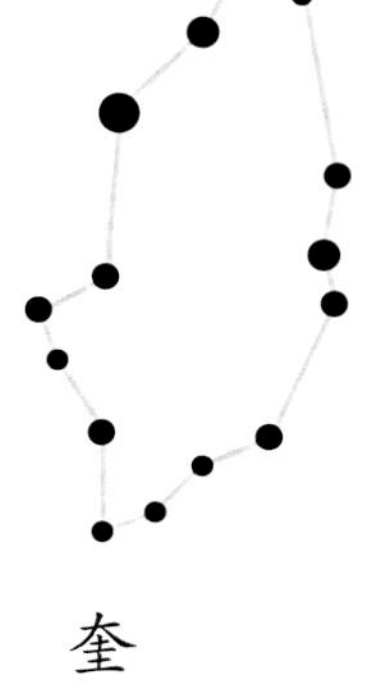

奎

觜

畢

參

THREE STARS
two rings
a newborn sun
tucked up
in the
corner
eye

There are
leaps for which
no NET appears
nor practiced
equations
enough to
hold up a
crumbling
bridge

Sewn
into the
STOMACH
lining
sorrow
autumns
into gold
ghost leaves
kiss the
astral
soil

My sun curls
into the warmth
of my crossed LEGS
pink knees and
elbows hang off
these aging edges
We are nothing
but two maps
overlapping
staving off
a slow
drift

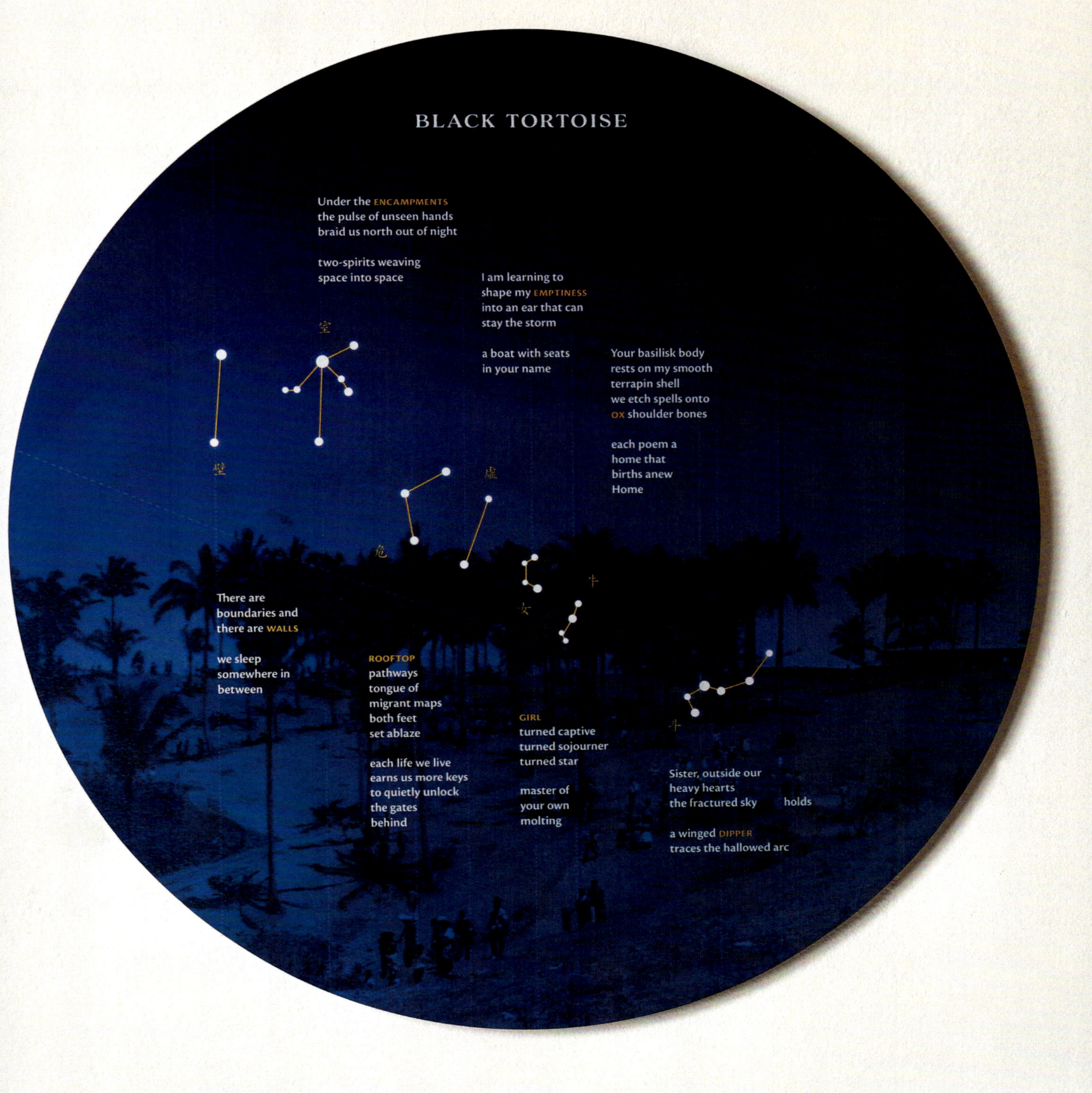

The Black Tortoise of the northern sky rules over seven mansions: Wall, Encampment, Rooftop, Emptiness, Girl, Ox, and Dipper. Associated with the season of winter and the element of water, they are a partnership of tortoise and snake closely entwined.

BLACK TORTOISE

Under the
ENCAMPMENTS
the pulse of unseen
hands
braid us north out of
night

two-spirits weaving
space into space

室

I am learning to
shape my
EMPTINESS
into an ear that can
stay the storm

a boat with seats
in your name

Your basilisk body
rests on my smooth
terrapin shell
we etch spells onto
ox shoulder bones

each poem a
home that
births anew
Home

壁

虛

There are
boundaries and
there are WALLS

we sleep
somewhere in
between

危

ROOFTOP
pathways
tongue of
migrant maps
both feet
set ablaze

each life we live
earns us more keys
to quietly unlock
the gates
behind

牛

女

GIRL
turned captive
turned sojourner
turned star

master of
your own
molting

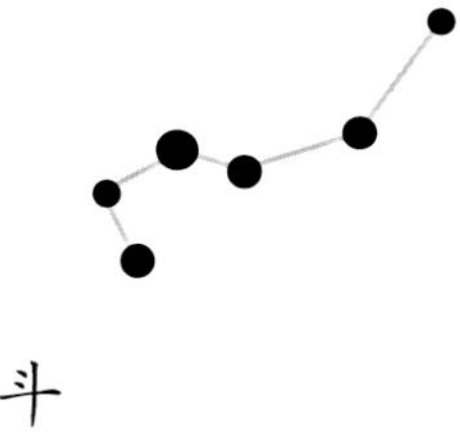

斗

Sister, outside our
heavy hearts
the fractured sky holds

a winged DIPPER
traces the hallowed arc

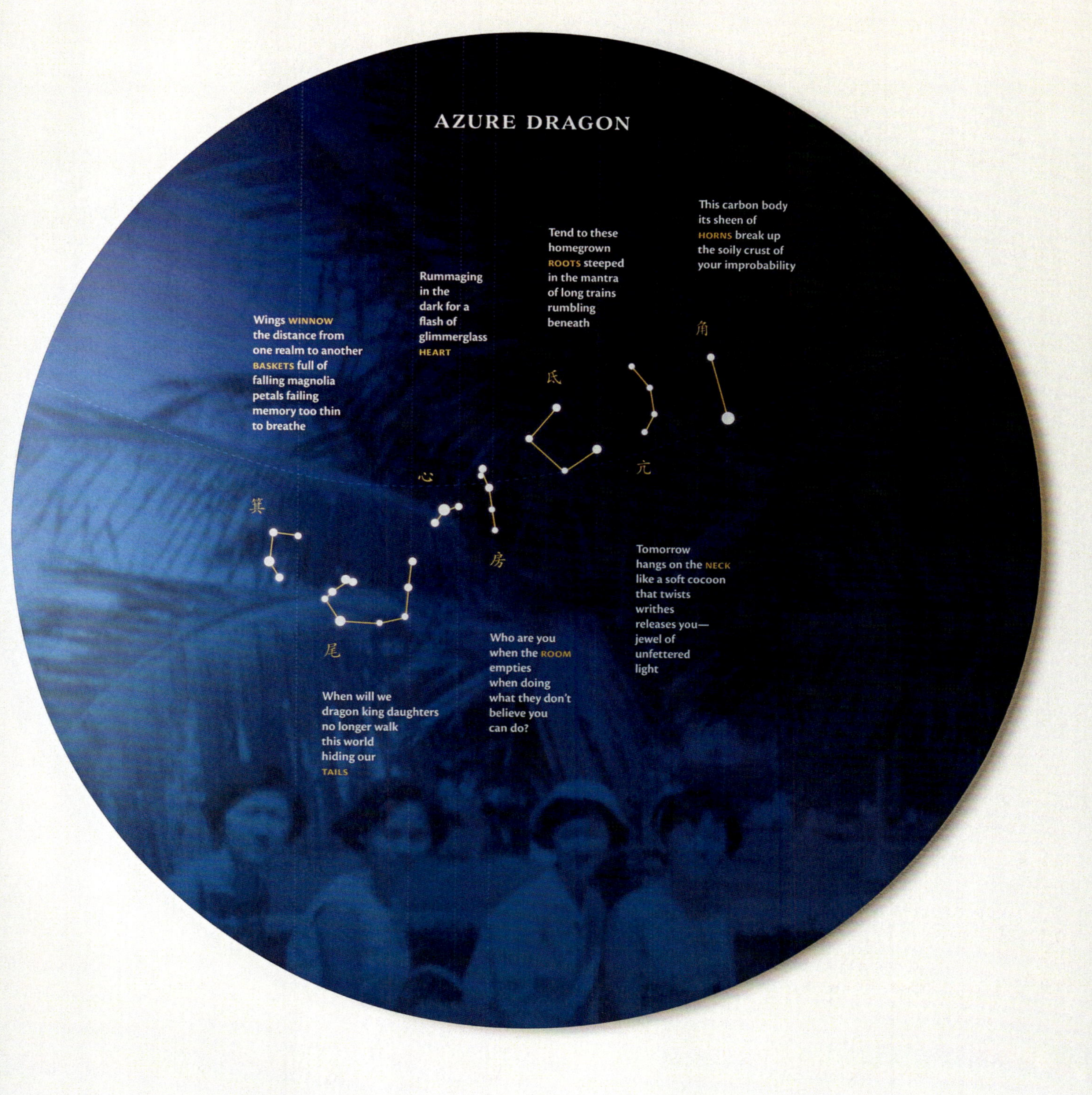

The Azure Dragon of the eastern sky rules over seven mansions: Winnow Basket, Tail, Heart, Room, Roots, Neck, and Horn. Associated with the season of spring and the element of wood, her wingspan extends seven generations forward and seven generations back.

AZURE DRAGON

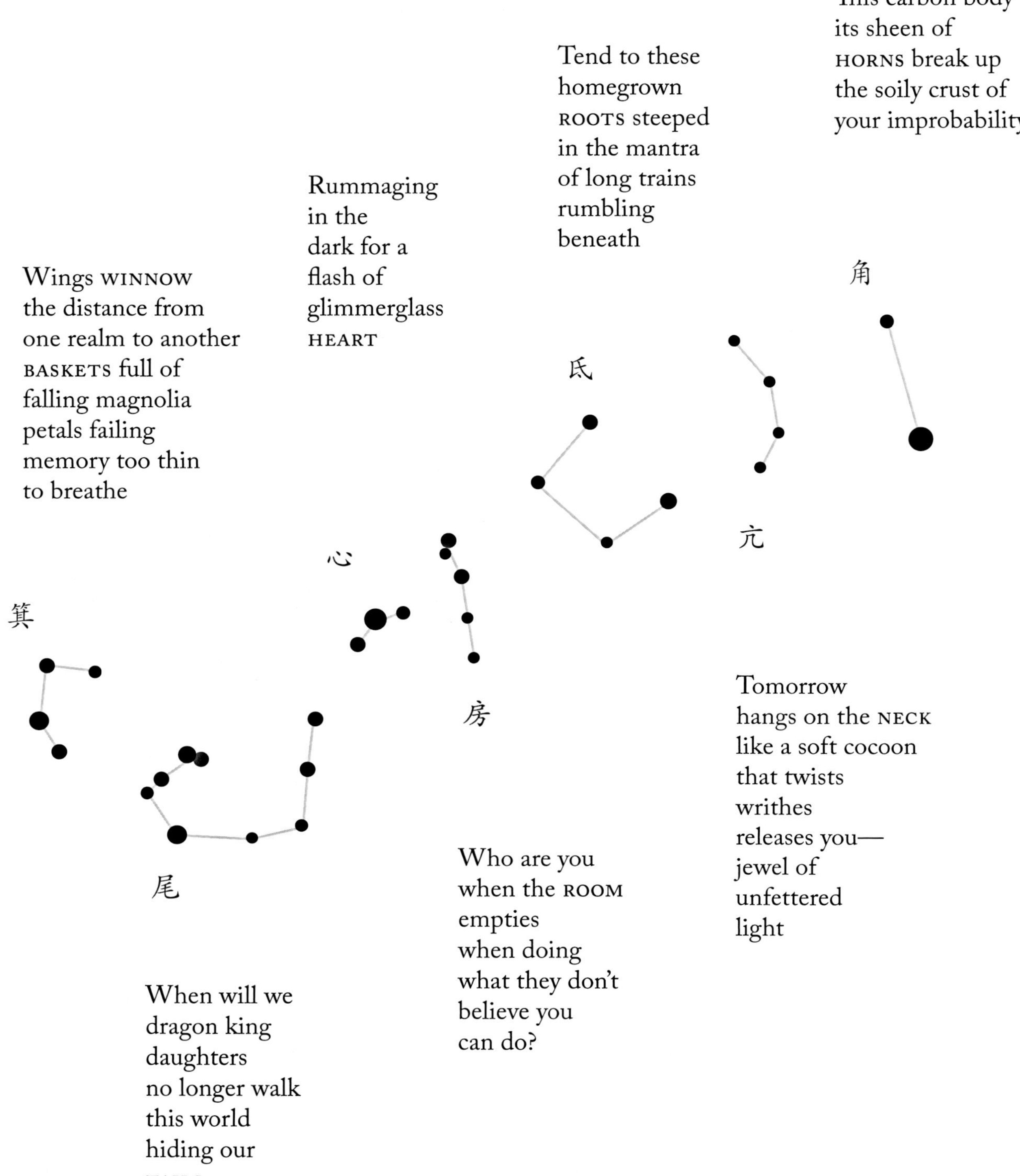

This carbon body
its sheen of
HORNS break up
the soily crust of
your improbability

Tomorrow
hangs on the NECK
like a soft cocoon
that twists
writhes
releases you—
jewel of
unfettered
light

Tend to these
homegrown
ROOTS steeped
in the mantra
of long trains
rumbling
beneath

Who are you
when the ROOM
empties
when doing
what they don't
believe you
can do?

Rummaging
in the
dark for a
flash of
glimmerglass
HEART

When will we
dragon king
daughters
no longer walk
this world
hiding our
TAILS

Wings WINNOW
the distance from
one realm to another
BASKETS full of
falling magnolia
petals failing
memory too thin
to breathe

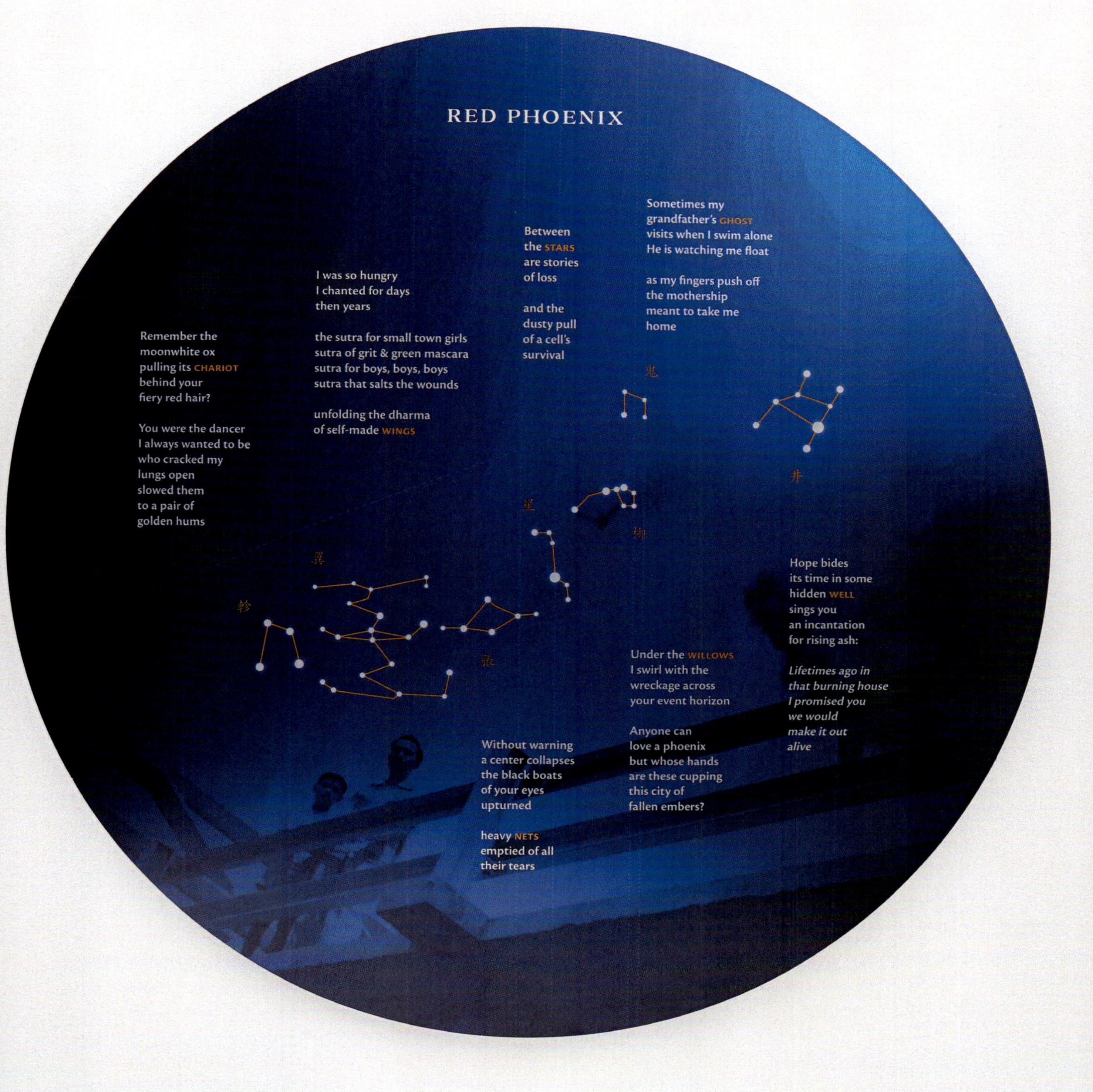

The Red Phoenix of the southern sky rules over seven mansions: Chariot, Wings, Net, Star, Willow, Ghost, and Well. Associated with the season of summer and the element of fire, she easily burns into the memory of closed eyes with her striking feathers.

RED PHOENIX

Remember the
moonwhite ox
pulling its CHARIOT
behind your
fiery red hair?

You were the dancer
I always wanted to be
who cracked my
lungs open
slowed them
to a pair of
golden hums

I was so hungry
I chanted for days
then years

the sutra for small town girls
sutra of grit & green mascara
sutra for boys, boys, boys
sutra that salts the wounds

unfolding the dharma
of self-made WINGS

Between
the STARS
are stories
of loss

and the
dusty pull
of a cell's
survival

Sometimes my
grandfather's GHOST
visits when I swim alone
He is watching me float

as my fingers push off
the mothership
meant to take me
home

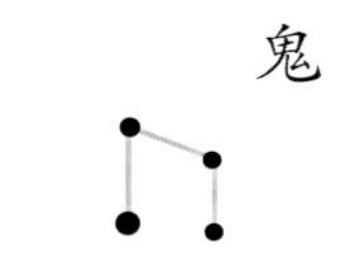

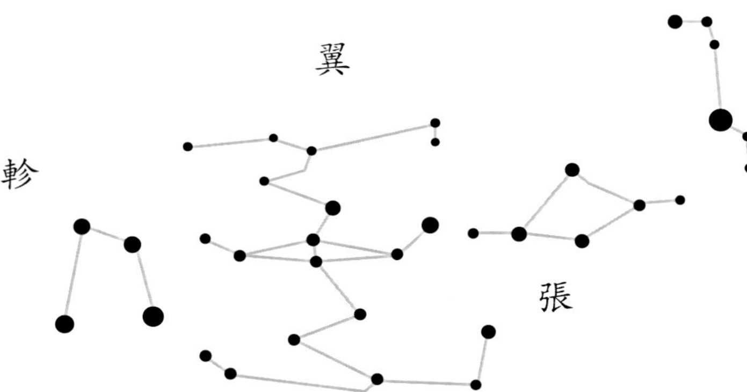

Without warning
a center collapses
the black boats
of your eyes
upturned

heavy NETS
emptied of all
their tears

Under the WILLOWS
I swirl with the
wreckage across
your event horizon

Anyone can
love a phoenix
but whose hands
are these cupping
this city of
fallen embers?

Hope bides
its time in some
hidden WELL
sings you
an incantation
for rising ash:

Lifetimes ago in
that burning house
I promised you
we would
make it out
alive

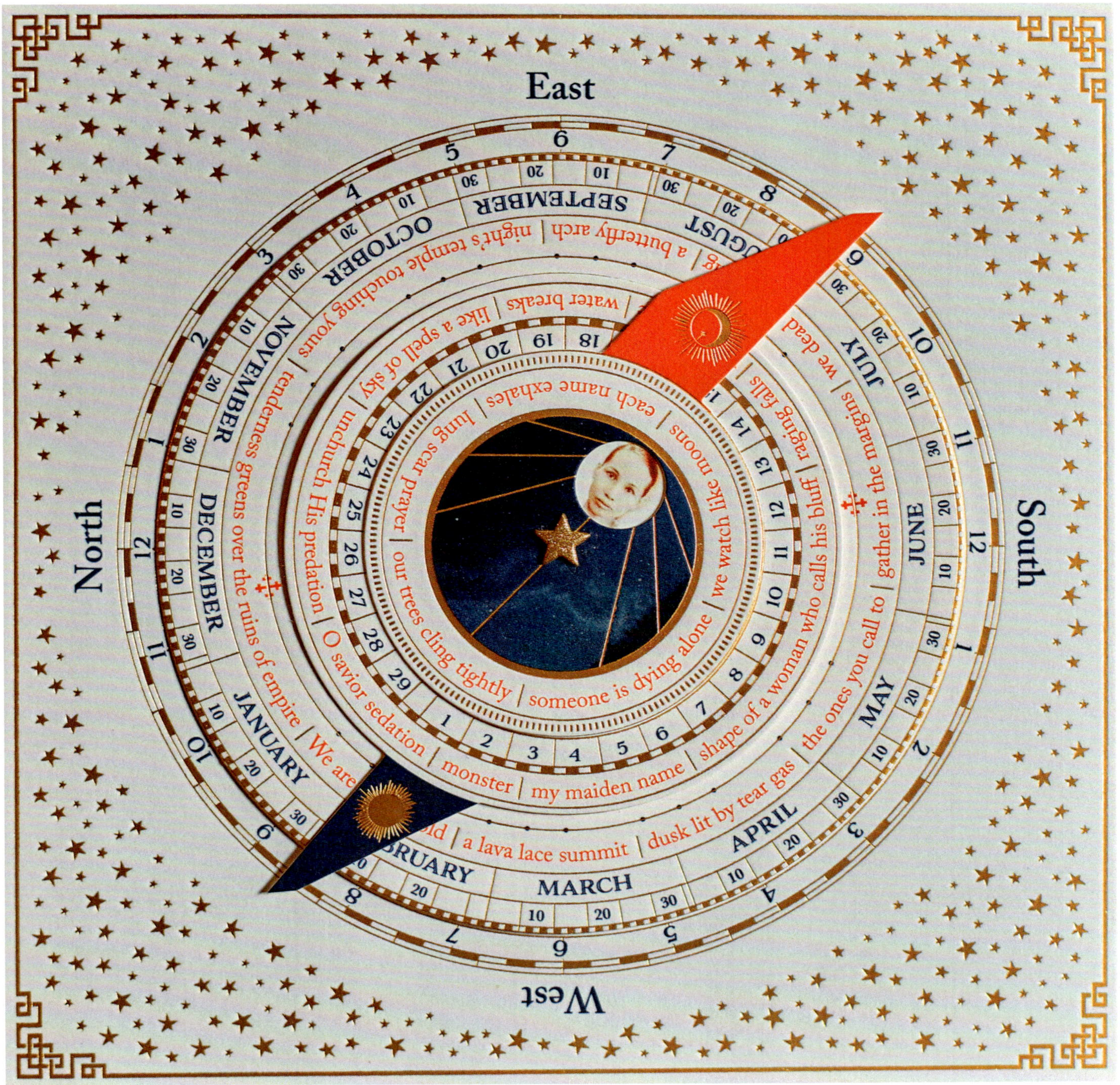

This interactive poem takes the form of a lunar volvelle. As the moon reveals its ever-changing shape, so too does the poem that radiates from the volvelle's heart. Fear not. During the full moon, my father's mother will watch over you.

LUNAR VOLVELLE

Each name exhales

water breaks
like a spell of sky

a butterfly arch
night's temple touching yours

lung scar prayer

unchurch His predation
O savior sedation

tenderness greens
over the ruins of empire

We are stronghold

Someone is dying alone

monster,
my maiden name

a lava lace summit
dusk lit by teargas

we watch like moons

shape of a woman who calls his bluff
raging falls

the ones you call to
gather in the margins

We dead awakening

** One possible reading of the poem during the full moon*

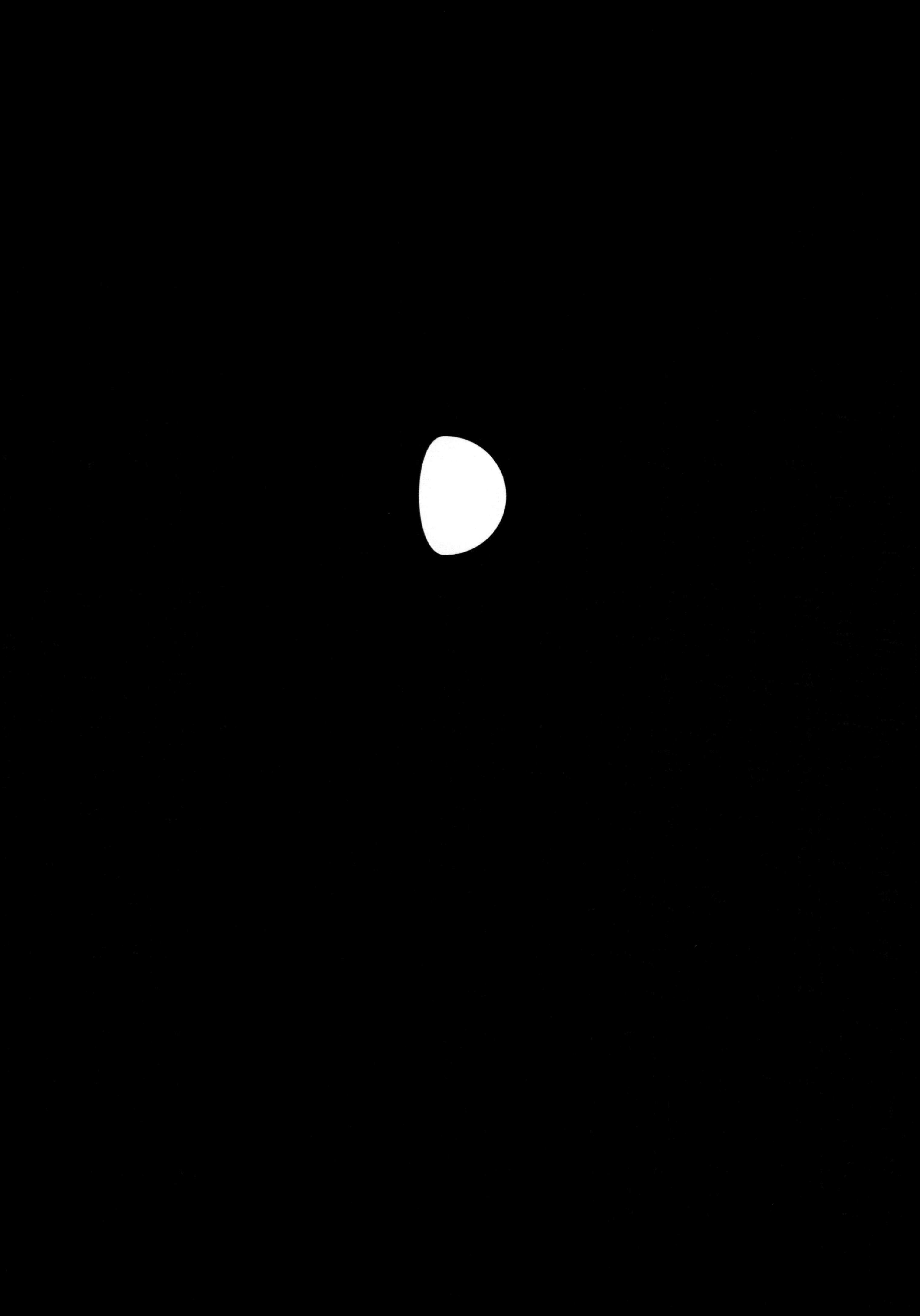

INDIGO INSOMNIA

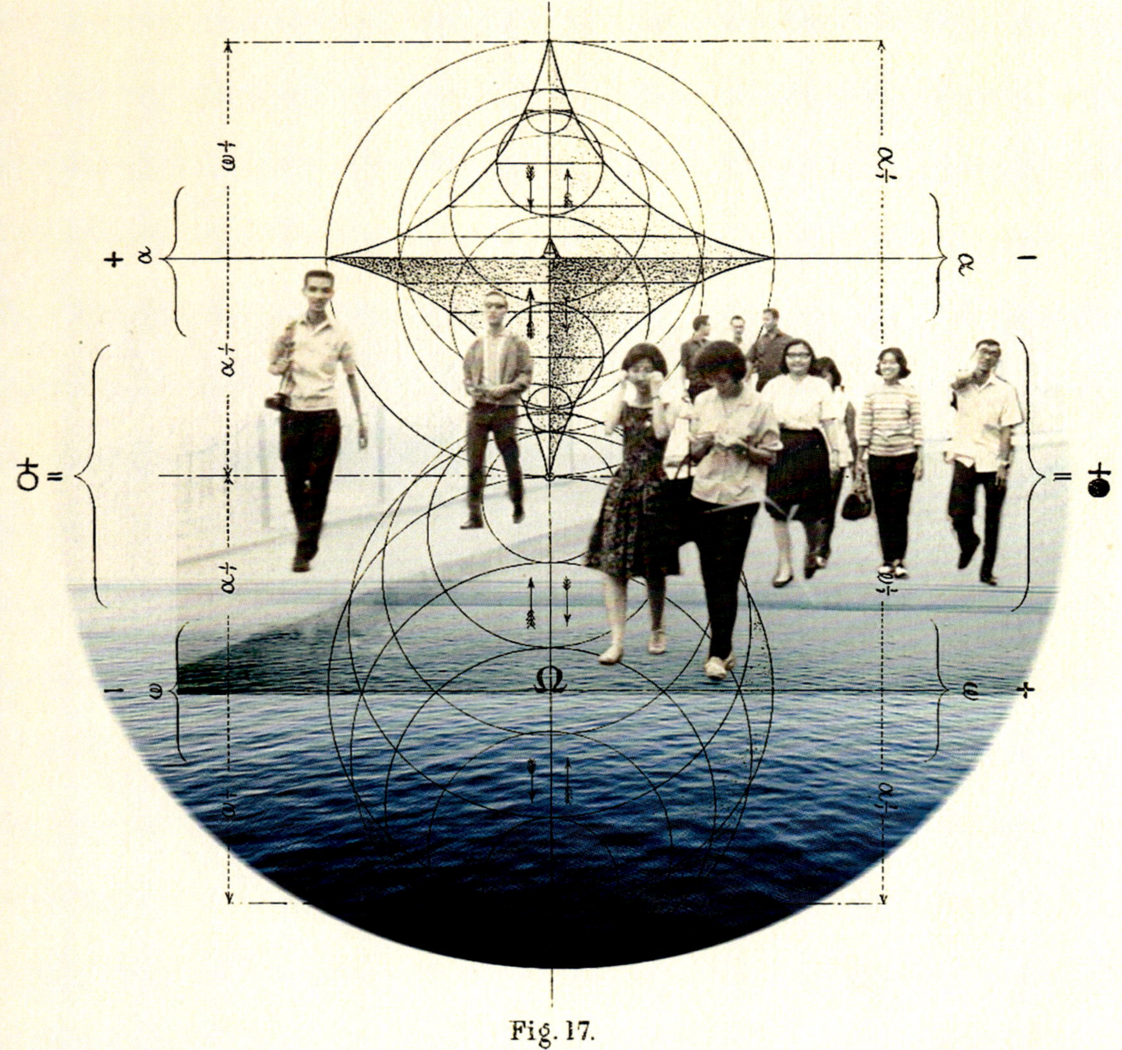

Fig. 17.

Indigo insomnia is a shrine of candles on the street corner of sudden absence, their dying strewn with flowers and handmade signs. Sleep, a scraggly stray, breathes with its tongue hanging low, sniffing each offering of dolls dampened by rain. Pauses. Then scurries into the alley towards the other side of amnesia.

Mother never told me my auntie's name was Juanita until she was near death, dying, or long dead. I can't remember. I called her by her title, Ah-Ching: as in Mother's Eldest Sister, as in Hidden Hurt, as in First Fire & Last Ember, as in Silent Shame Waiting Behind the Trees.

We say the names of the dead more often in afterlife than during the departed's lifetime. Indigo insomnia is the great waking, this birthing of the world anew. *From the indigo, an even deeper blue*, it is said. Perhaps this is why father hardly slept my entire childhood. His thin frame disappearing into the long white lab coat. A small square photo of my face in one pocket, and a black pager in the other, both blinking as he walked his rounds until the gray blue dawn.

The mouth holds many things except the language of the new, still forming between the lungs. The spoken vow we breathe, but don't yet know how to defend. Scrolling through the phone, one sees mostly ghosts or the self, ghosted, an accounting of strings stretched and broken. Someone slightly out of tune. Wondering if your voice is in the wrong chord, the wrong song, the wrong language, or just a painting of the ocean, its roar muted by a gilded gaze that sees but doesn't listen.

Indigo insomnia is diving into the deepest waters of memory to uncover the bodies hidden by our bad inheritance. My anxious study of patterns and vertices that squint for a brand new design. It is to know that there are no saviors except for that one decision standing outside your screen door. During the pandemic, brown paper packages pile up on the front porch like an avalanche of grievances. Time slows down so we can notice. Every person I pass on the street walks with an abandoned child clinging on their backs. I look into those round, wet eyes and my mouth feels the same hunger, dry and gritty with ocean salt.

The problem with numbers that count our deaths is that they don't carry the smell of moss or fresh cut grass from the bottom of your brother's shoes. They easily forget that one is sometimes two, that bitter melons are actually sweet if you eat them far from home. You cannot hear the hours of static nor the quiet breathing of your mother swirling in clouds of dirty rice water between the long wet grains and your cold fingertips moving in circles. This is why it is called lossy data.

Indigo insomnia is the truth asking for a ring in her latest ultimatum. It is stillness acknowledging the injuries painted over by the flag or a blight of bronze. The mass grave of bodies that rise beneath Christmas snow. Their cause of death and elaborate cover up, one in the same. In school we call it History, enshrine terror in red, white, and blue ribbons that we wear in our permed hair to match summer's twirling dresses. Orchestrated fires pop across the black body of July's night sky. Children gather to lick patriotic popsicles named after the bomb.

SYZYGY

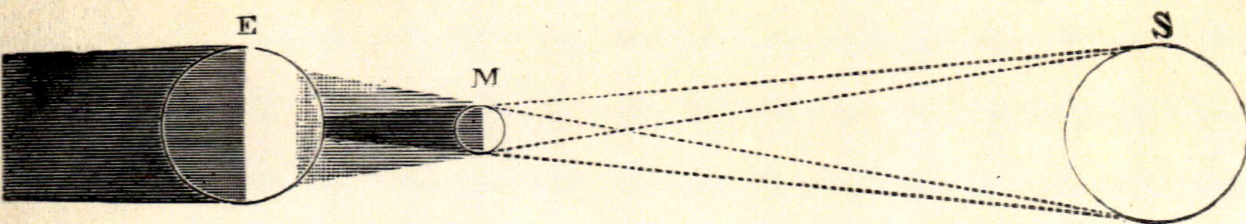

Fig. 1. — Total Eclipse of the Sun.
When is a son no longer a son?
We look up unable to recognize our kin. Bloodlines severed by a single vote.
How easily stories get fastened onto bodies. How black they bleed against—

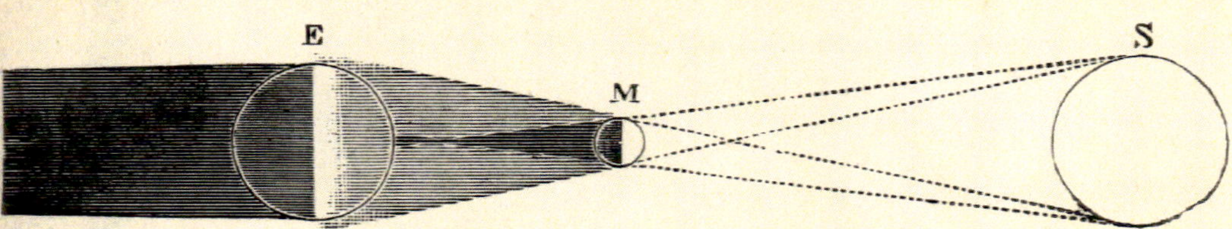

Fig. 2. — Annular Eclipse of the Sun.
I place banana leaves onto grandmother's lids. My piety thin as pressed flowers.
The sun is pushing us all outside our skin casings. Closer to the sky.

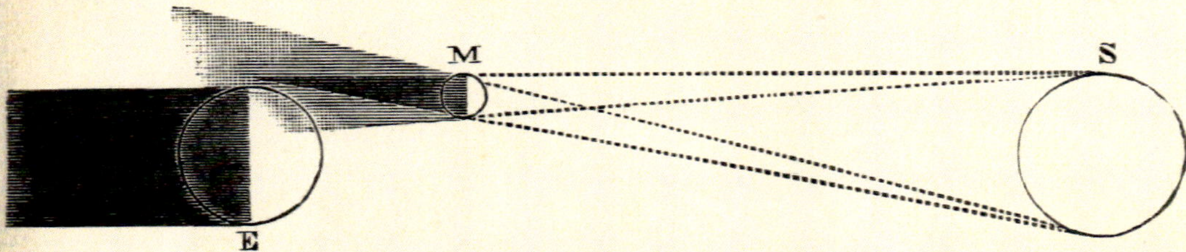

Fig.3. — Partial Eclipse of the Sun.
When is a daughter no longer a daughter?
Penumbra, a finger touched eye. We live entire worlds beyond a mother's periphery.
Without diagnosis, hers is a path of totality. We just want to be seen.

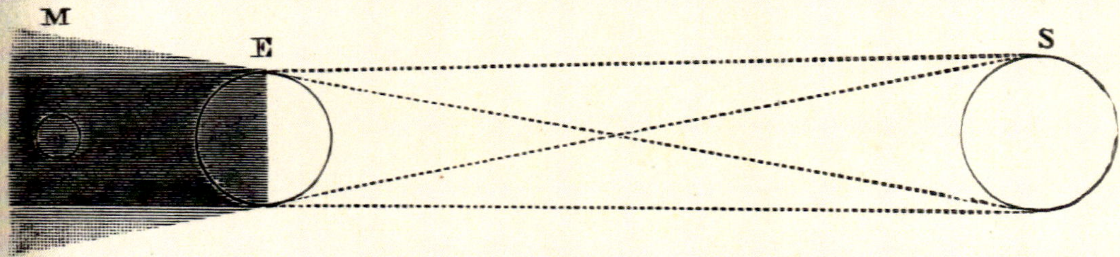

Fig.4. — Total Eclipse of the Moon.
My rooms are filled with your darkness, empty and unkempt. The umbra's edge.
Anywhere I look is light reflected. A knife that never touches you.

HER HYPOTHESIS

The foregoing deduction of her hypothesis was in the way she clicked her tongue at you for having *only* one baby, for not doing God's work, though you didn't know that you were working for a man, your body clocked in for some disembodied boss, that it was written in the contract of these contractions, that this was somehow your performance for a deified director, where you are already failing the auditions. Further study would show her that this assumption might be so far from correct if only the sharp sound of her tongue did not snap you back in place, at least for a little while, sitting in the dressing room going over your lines again and again. Your timing is off, the writing sloppy, and for whatever reason no one can hear you no matter how loud you try to project. Lines are being drawn in the sandbox and relatively speaking everywhere you stand is marked upstage. Binary and other double stars and star clusters gather over lattes during the day, while you are working your office job to save up enough vacation time at the end of the year in order to labor over a few flimsy poems. To show exactly on what considerations a change of view is founded, you recall the tall pines from long walks with Sylvia's ghost who keeps asking you for directions. How you keep shrugging like you do in the kitchen whenever your son asks what the difference is between boys and girls. Like the kitchen lights and B-movie scripts, your inclination is to flip them off and upside down, to lift the curtain from the stage. But such irregularities are very frequent, and it would lead to an obvious absurdity to explain them on her terms, that you realize you don't need to explain anything to anyone, that you actually only work for women directors these days, specifically the ones who have not yet been born, that you are not in the business of best-selling scripts but prefer the intimacy of a one-woman show, spinning in the dark with your little one's candied squeal and sticky fingers as you come up for air in this last revolution of laughter before we all fall down.

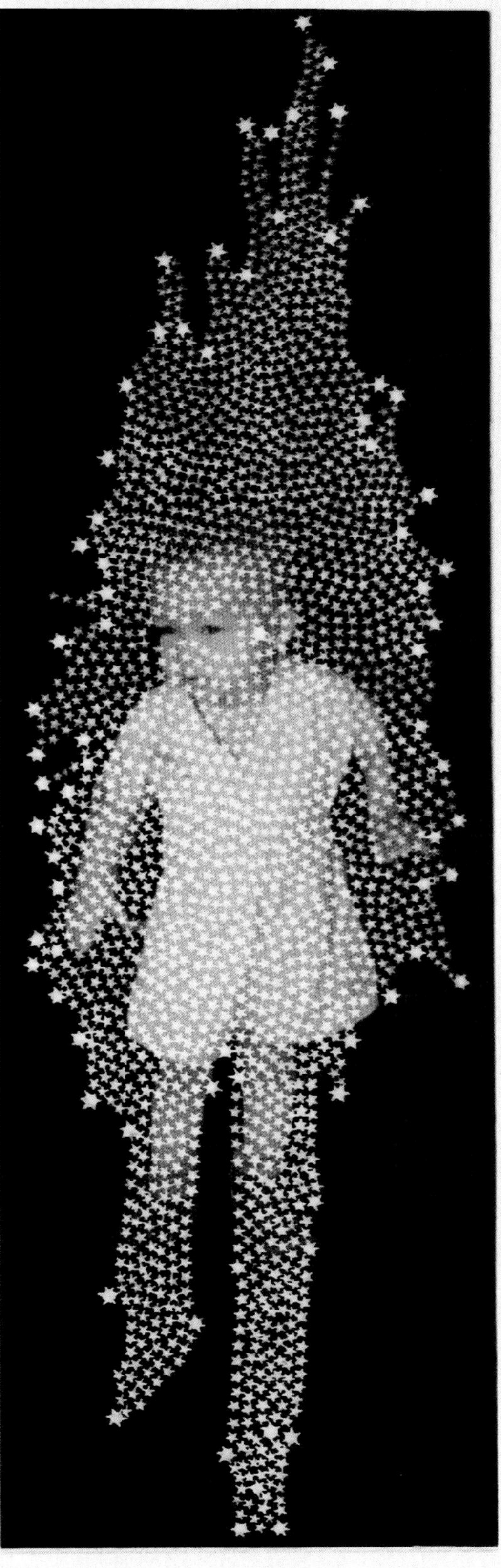

Fig. 109.—After Herschel's view of the form of the universe.

WOMAN'S PLACE IN THE UNIVERSE

Are you not convinced,
Daughters can also be heroic?

—Wang Zhenyi (1768-1797)

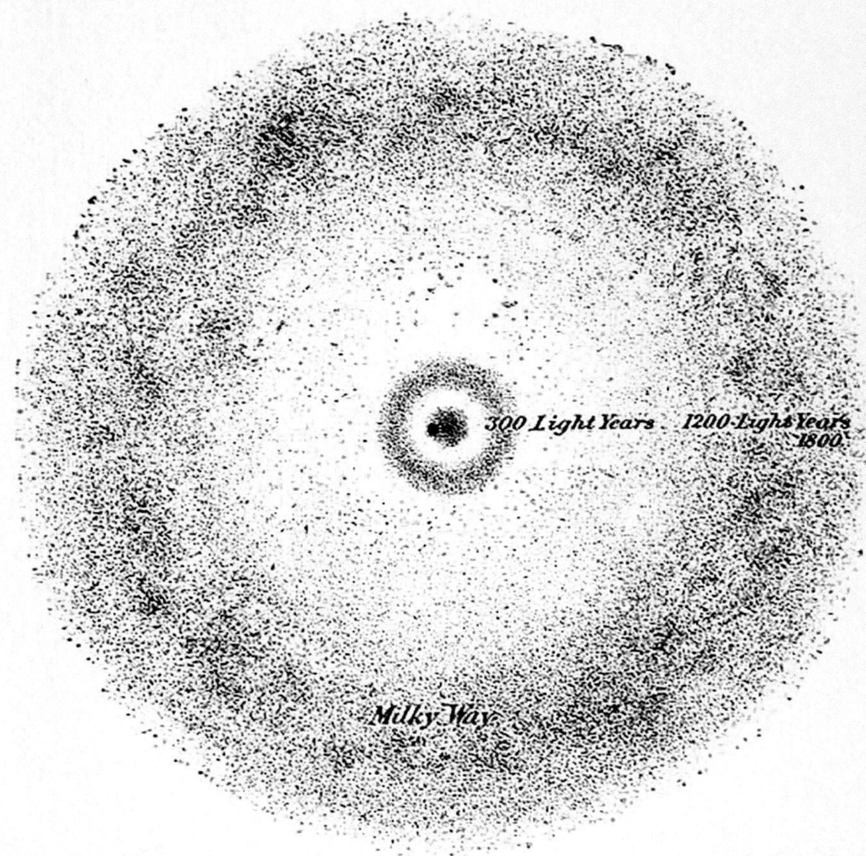

Odd number. Odd girl. One is an observation. The other, a polite indictment. She preferred to arrange her studio against the laws of symmetry, her way of saying *up yours* to Confucius and his man-pandering precepts. No matching pillows, tilted walls, her father's books all perfect bound yet bent like a wormwood granny's feet.

Imagine a woman's calculations opening up the sky, the sun's orbit but a mole on the lip of solar clustered nipple. How she spilled the milk from the glass of her astronomer eye knowing it would feed another hunger in another womb of time.

Mathematics were just foreplay. There is nothing wrong with being easy. Any man can scribble odes to flatter a goddess of the moon. She turned her garden into a laboratory to decipher the secret turning of the stars. Behind the ecliptic strung up crystal, she glimpsed her face in the lunar mirror's gleam.

Infinite planets. Her endless ether. There are those whose greatness grows in shadow, whose outer limits the spotting of blood cannot contain.

WHO WILL GIVE YOU HAIRCUTS ON MARS

PLATE II

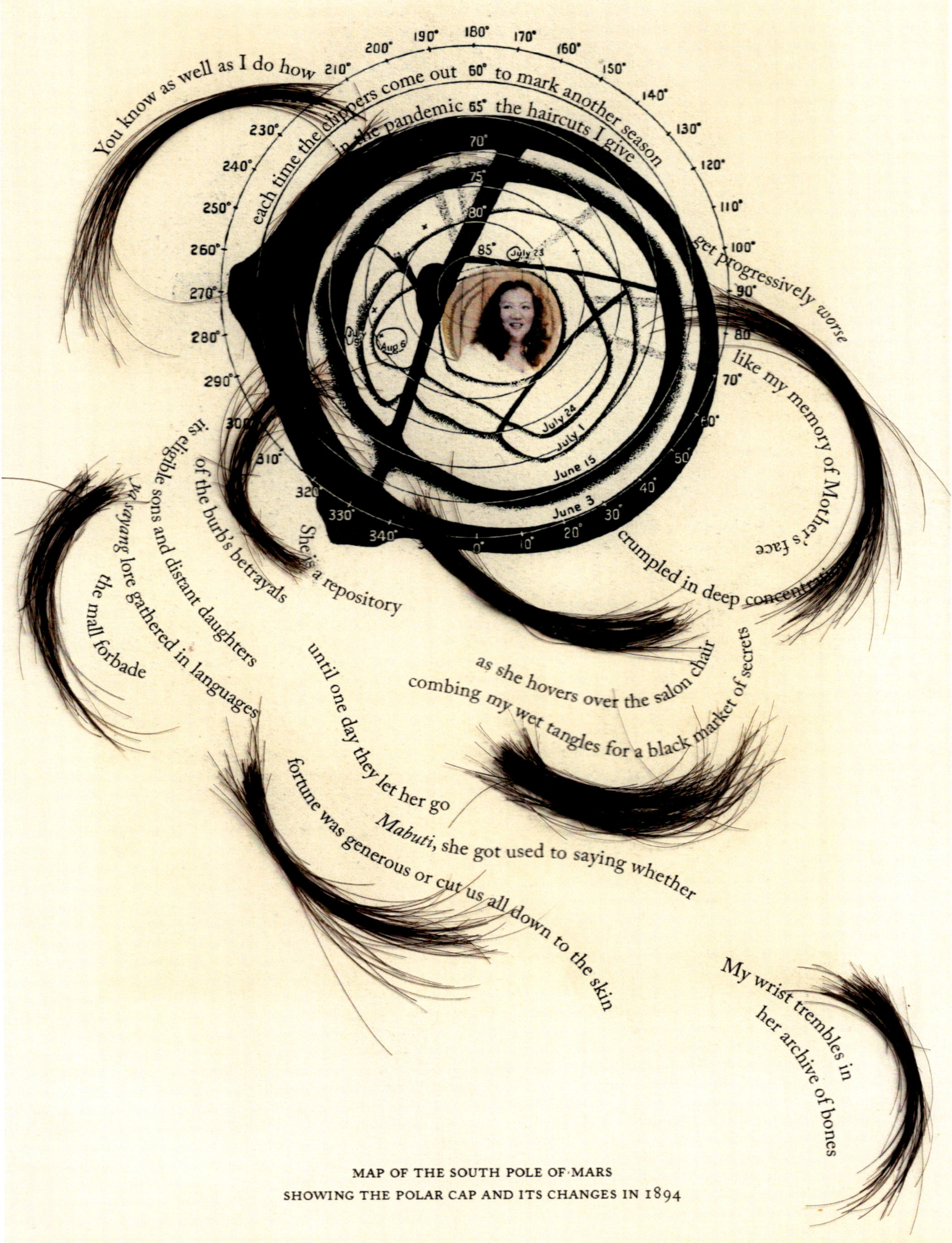

MAP OF THE SOUTH POLE OF MARS
SHOWING THE POLAR CAP AND ITS CHANGES IN 1894

WHO WILL GIVE YOU HAIRCUTS ON MARS

You know as well as I do how
each time the clippers come out
to mark another season in the pandemic
the haircuts I give get progressively
worse

like my memory of Mother's face
crumpled in deep concentration
as she hovers over the salon chair
combing my wet tangles
for a black market of secrets

She is a repository of the burb's betrayals
its eligible bachelors and distant daughters
ya sayang lore gathered in languages
the mall forbade until one day
they let her go

Mabuti, she got used to saying
whether fortune was generous or
cut us all down to the skin
My wrist trembles in
her archive of bones

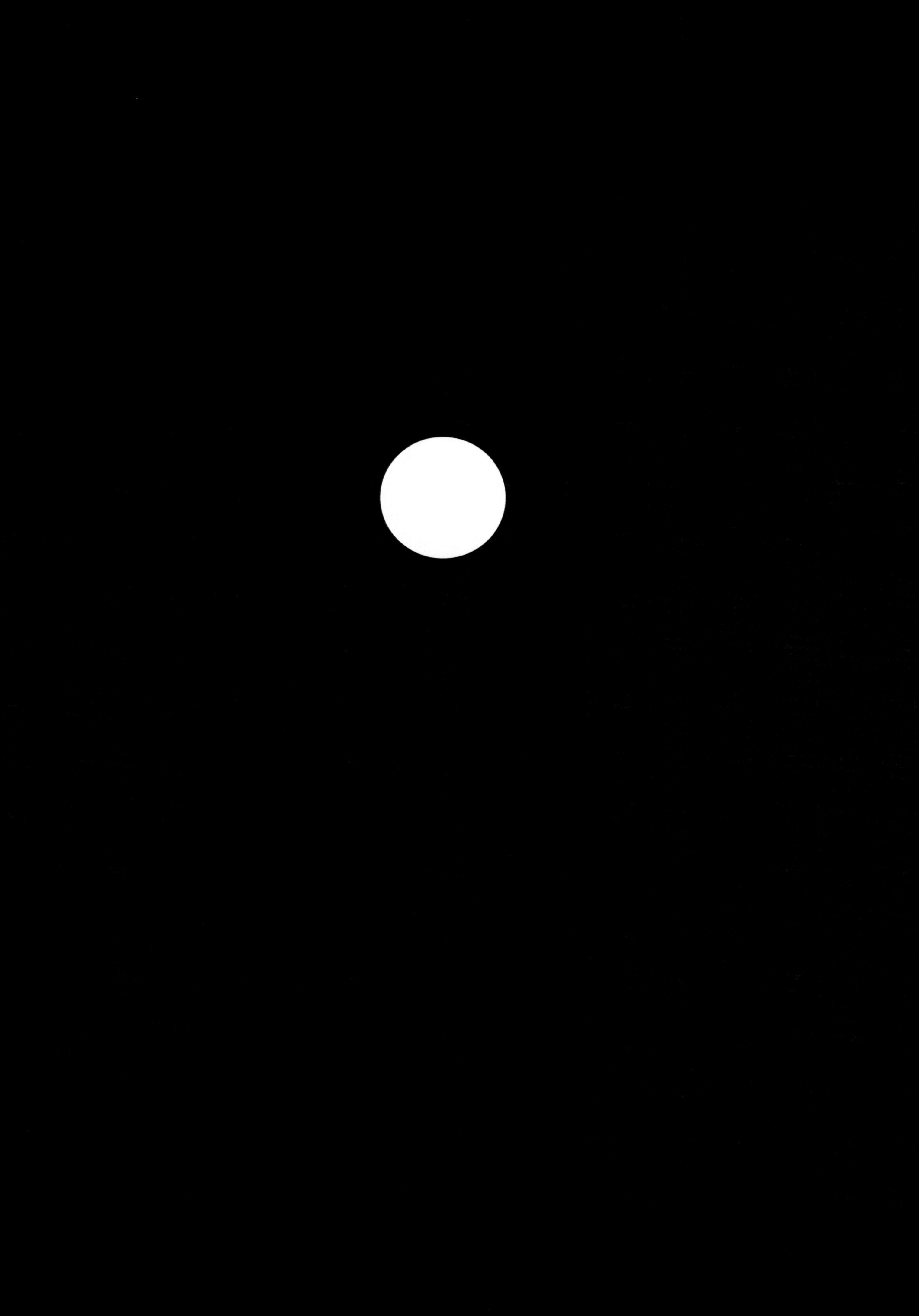

SANGUINE INSOMNIA

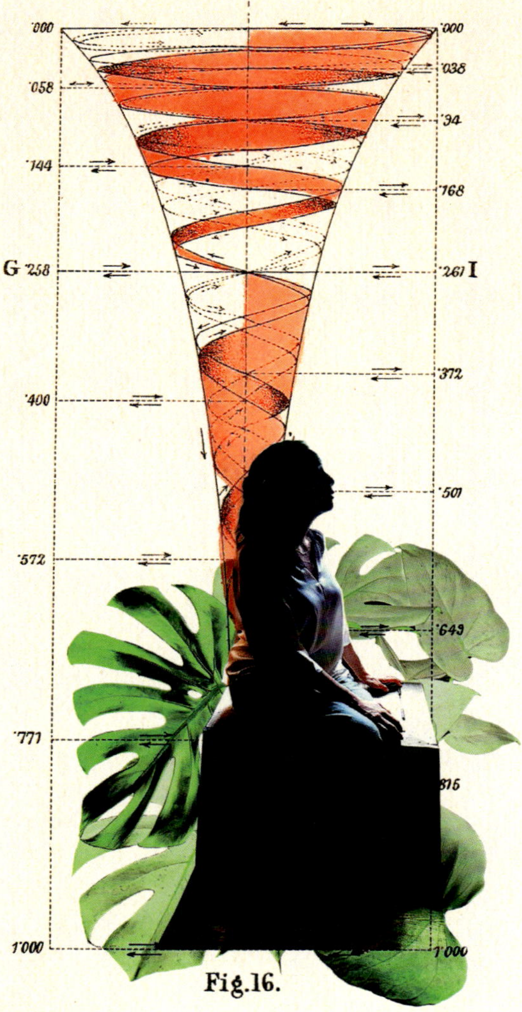

Fig.16.

Sanguine insomnia is a coil of indeterminateness, still warm with blood, that winds through the gray areas—where no one is looking—your body an empty lot of broken words buried beneath hot asphalt. Spiral lines encircle your swollen hands, stung by swarms of small print, these parasitic alphabets arranged for the most elegant of thefts: your labor, your time, your space, until you are nothing more than a hairline crack on gentrified pavement where trees are trimmed to trunk. The sweltering sun gives strikers no choice but to go home. The door, you are told, will open only *after* they hang your face on their storefront windows, feed on you until you run dry, making sure to take the bread out of your baby's mouth to sop up all the sauce.

No is the moment we stop bleeding sleep. No to gas lights dimming the way. No more give, no forgiving—they always meant for you to give in. That half-baked loaf of exposure: you're conditioned to covet every crumb. How would it feel to survive without suffering? To taste bitters sweeten as they eat out of your hands? We all dream of living beyond these white walls, in evergreen orchards of our own making. Where branches sway, bow to you, heavy with red moon apples.

FEATHER

Primal fire burns on feathered bone. Ink blots billow into a milk-strewn sky, curving to the traffic of car streak stars. Crickets sing you deep into the dark, the vaulted doors of open eyes crack wide. Come. Nestle in the kinship of our gorgeous insignificance.

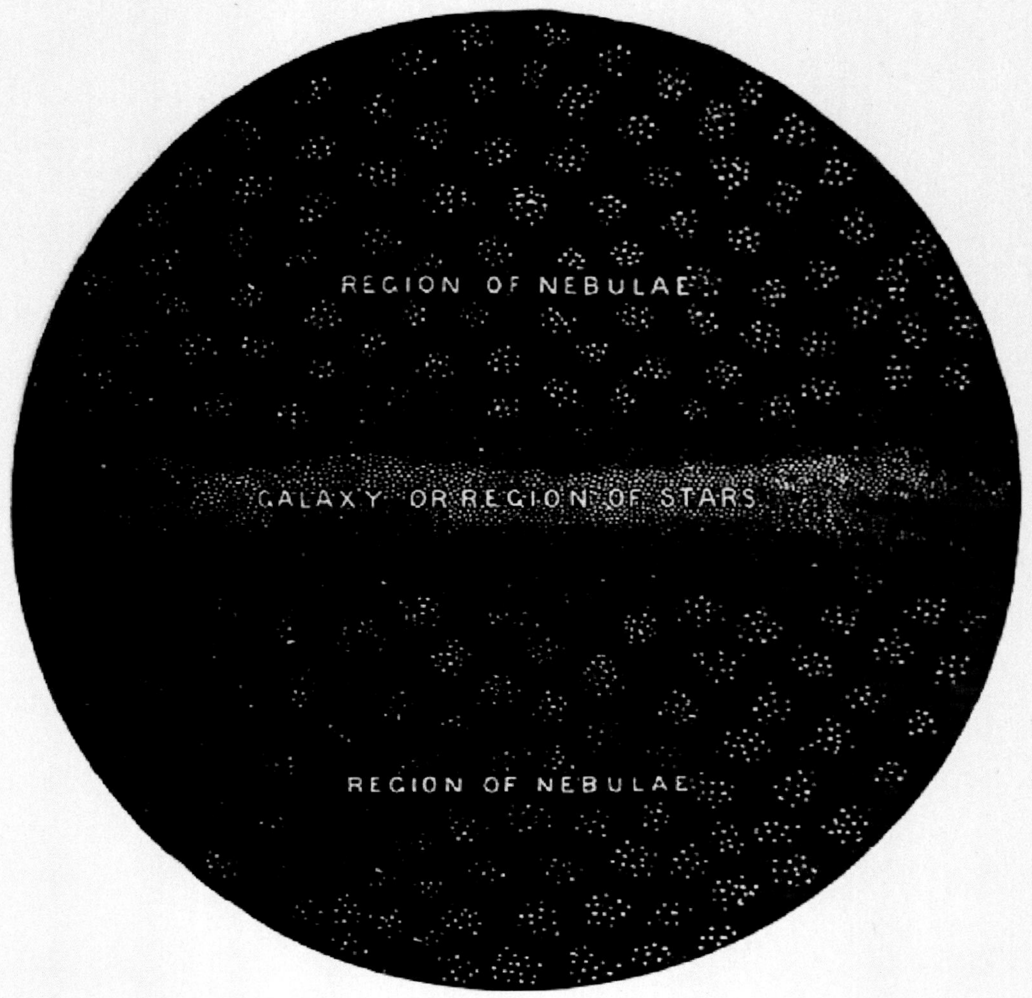

Take comfort in knowing that this year is but a blink in the breath of trees and cosmic moss, that the nebulae with all their dust hardly noticed how the phone slowly died, how you burned the maps to your forefathers' graves. The gaze is turning toward unborn cities.

These wounds won't outlive Jupiter's eye, its red stare fixed on a three-hundred-year storm. To look is to choose. To see, to sea the primordial stew of trial and error and error and error. Cosmonauts wear loneliness like a bear's back against the night, softly.
The exoplanets have no sympathy; they've been at it for years.

You float yourself over this tiny dot, aglow in its mobile bluing. Glimmer in the sweet dusk of amber with its powdered resin in your nose. Maybe we can speak again.

SUN, NOT SON

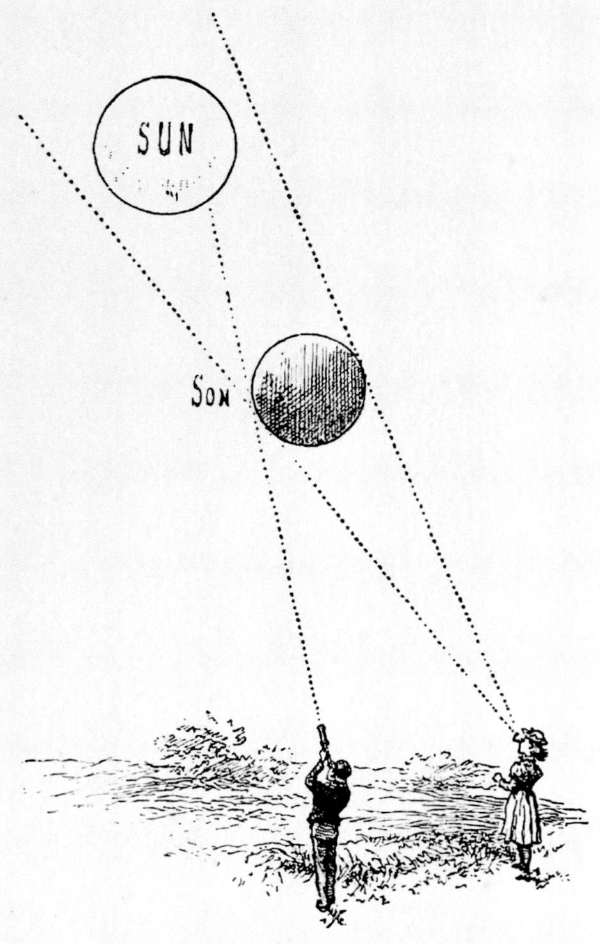

I prefer to say *sun*, not *son* with an *o*. That car crash of gender falls silent on these ears. Each new day is written with this young dwarf star, burning little body, curled on milky belly or sometimes nestled in my dark pits of unsatisfying sleep.

My sun wakes, pretends to be a sleeping beauty waiting to be kissed into morning's golden choir. Upon rising, the sun makes my coffee and asks if we can paint together on rocks, paper, finger nails, dawning all things equally with delight. The sun likes most things hot except for honey tea, which is always served lukewarm.

The other son remains spelled with a closed loop and at times the stony stare of a pent-up gun barrel. It is a hole that leads to another hole, an inheritance of bottomless hunger. It rattles, wondering what to eat, who to own, where to sink, this newsfeed of gravity pulling us all down, asking: What does it mean to be a man?

My sun prefers the shape of a donut after taking that first powdered bite. We gaze at the wingtips of geese undulating gently in the silvered winter sky. If we are lucky, a crescent moon, stroked by my sun's long black lashes and the curve of arms flung up—as if to set free—something that believes in flight.

BLOOD MOON WOMAN

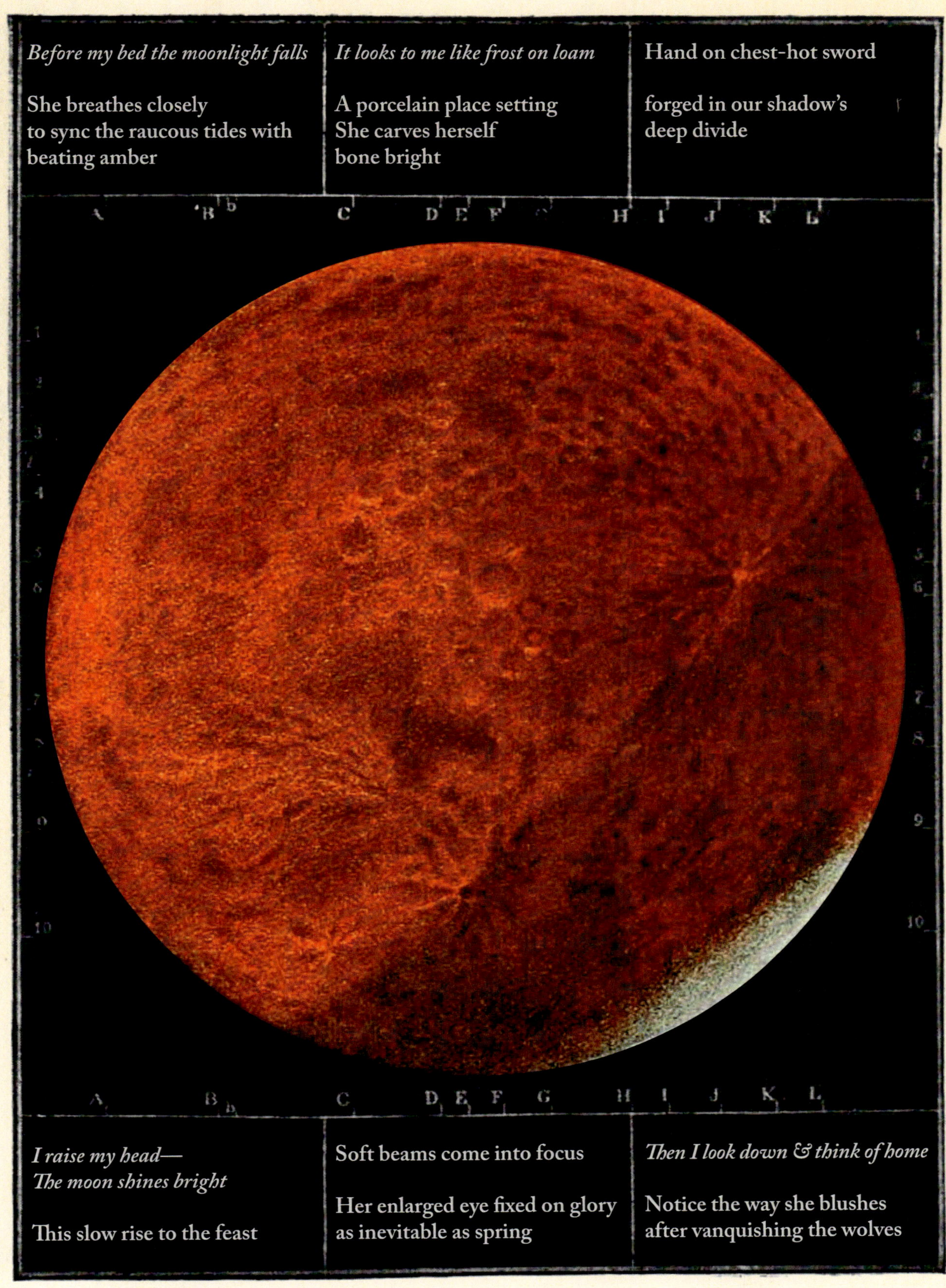

With lines from "Quiet Night Thought" by Li Bai (701-762)

BOOK OF VERA

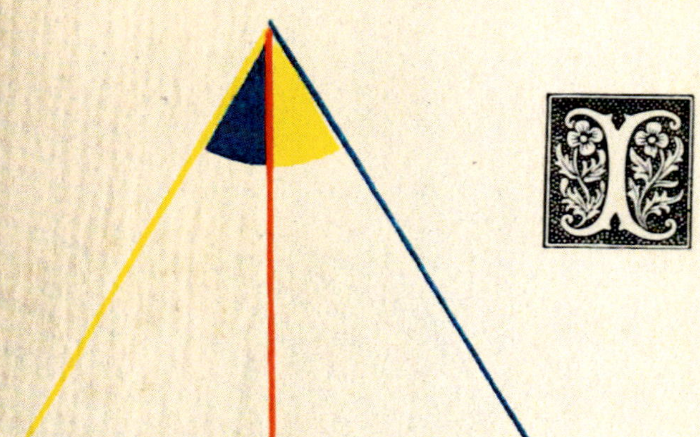

In the mid-1960s, Vera Rubin was granted access to San Diego's prestigious Palomar Observatory, an old boys' club so infamous astronomers called it "the monastery." Though she could use the telescope, Rubin was informed that there was nowhere for her to relieve herself—the facility had no women's restroom.

To enter a room is to perforate the stark white page
optical precision sharp as the inner edge of arms wide open
(I was a girl born to be a shadow)

The first point is to begin ( ), to split open the fiber of the field
cut your teeth on curved starlight and lonely work
(What does it feel like to be the only, where none before you came?)

The second is to pivot ( ), steady the blade as far as you can go
They will keep telling you not to go there, that the room has no room
Notice how the doors are spelled, how distant

(How did you do it with four moons in your orbit?)
Their little bodies call you by your other name:
Mother, a generous garden that spreads forth onto long wide tables

As the pulp of years give way to the shape of genius
you make a turn, circumnavigate a single point ( )

Your sun's gown pours onto the hot glass,
tilted towards a spectra of galaxies, burning

Spirals of testimony agree with you about the missing girls
unseen hands that knead the dough, fold the cloth, hold us down,
their resistance a safeguard from the senseless spinning out of sight

(I slip your triangle into the lining of my inner pocket)

Beneath this concentrated scowl, I am a girl searching ( )
for the observatory bathroom, echoing the hallway where you firmly pressed
onto the door a cutout paper skirt and said:

There you go; now you have a ladies' room.

SHOOTING STARS

The path of the mother crossing the child's track is not fixed but an improvised tune, a thin voice unraveling herself from tip to end towards this new needle's hidden eye. First lips then a name, and from there a continuous line that fluctuates in bursts and plumes of haze. Her orbital eccentricity is littered with glitter-glue stuck in the most forsaken places: beneath car seats, in wild tangles of hair, or the tuck of stinky little toes. It follows that the orbit in which the mother is revolving undergoes persistent change; the path she follows in

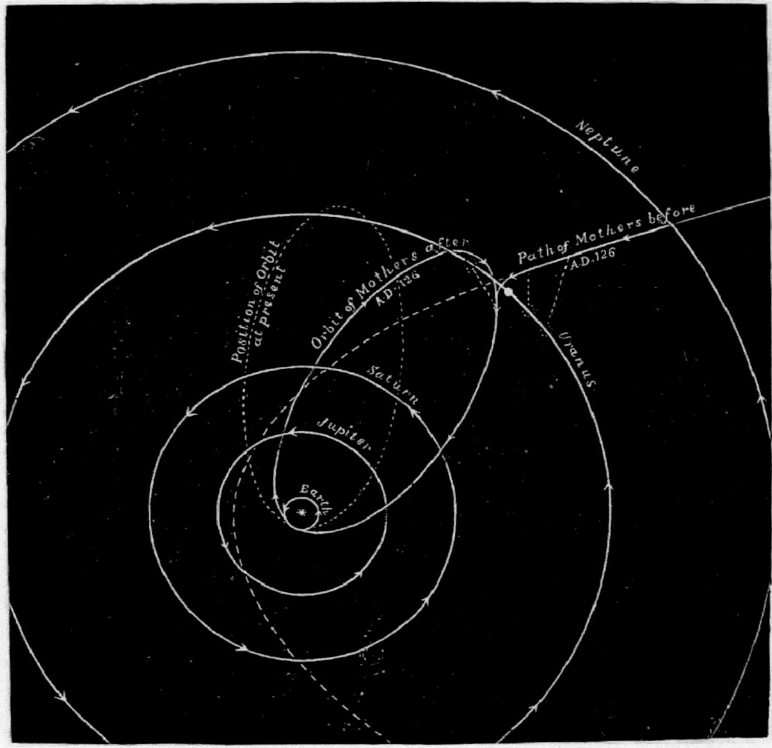

one revolution will never look like another's, though during her long commutes through asphalt and steel she may feel deep down like everyone else, that she is lost, not exactly sure what she is doing but listening, tuning herself to her child's higher register whose call rings at the top of each day. Sometimes she stands on the dotted perimeter of a bouncy birthday party where nobody will speak to her, arising uneasy speculation about whether she might actually be an exoplanet among these social systems, waving her tiny arms like an ant light-years away. The mother takes comfort when her body pulls close to her little star as she passes in front of his door, his heat pulsing in her swollen heart. Yet the horizon holds days when he will drift towards the outer rim his faint glow glinting in her weakening eyes. What light will he bring to those dark distances? On whose sky will he paint his signature shower of starling gloss? Even she knows she cannot decide the trajectory of august dreams, not the color of blossoms nor the shape of trees, nothing she can do to code her calculations into the arbitrary algorithm of karma's pact with time. She just wants him to know that she will be there at each successive return where they will cross at a point about a half degree further on in the direction in which he is traveling, where she'll be holding up bright neon signs, packing sliced jazz apples in ziploc bags, wearing an oversized t-shirt in his name.

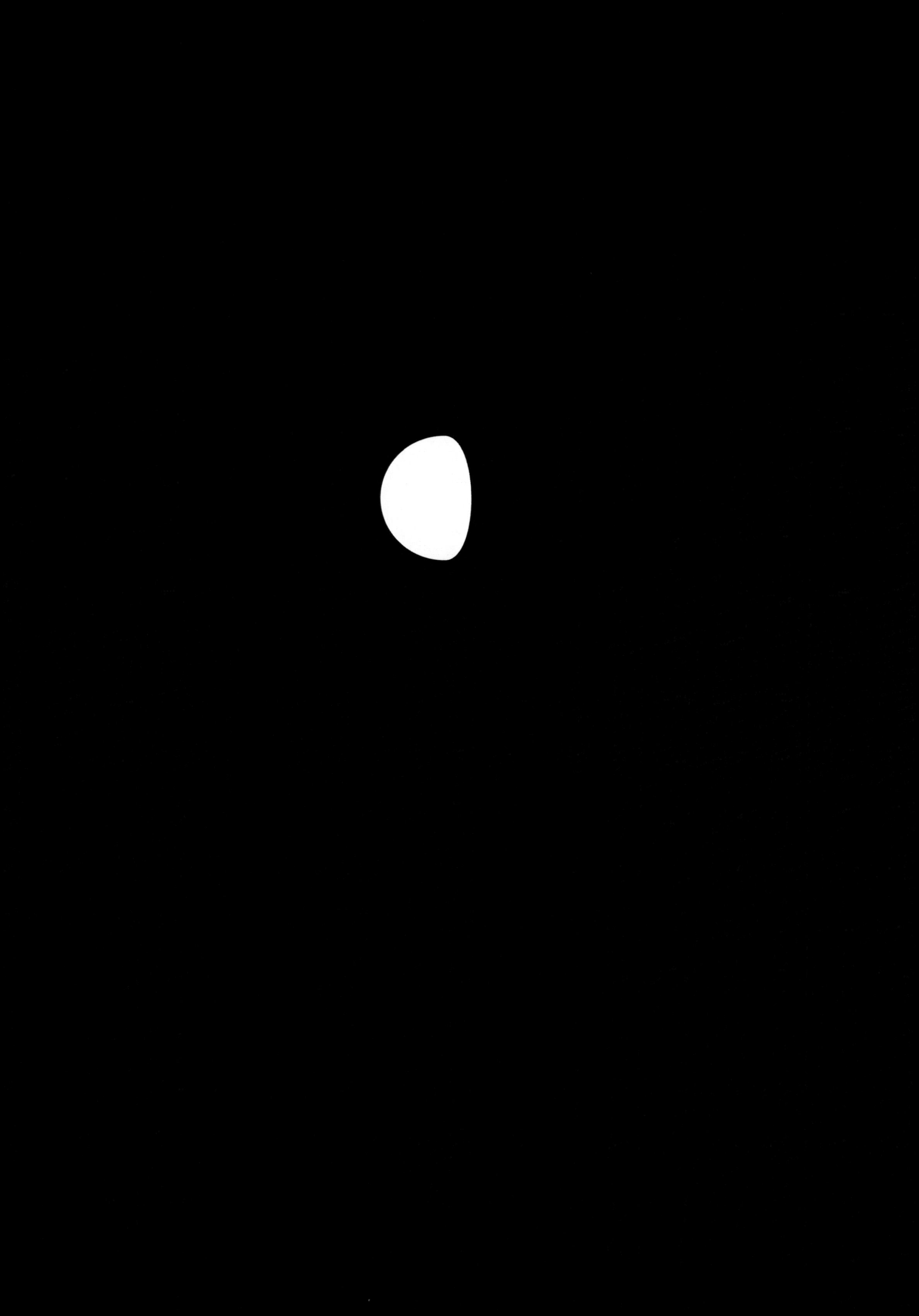

JADE INSOMNIA

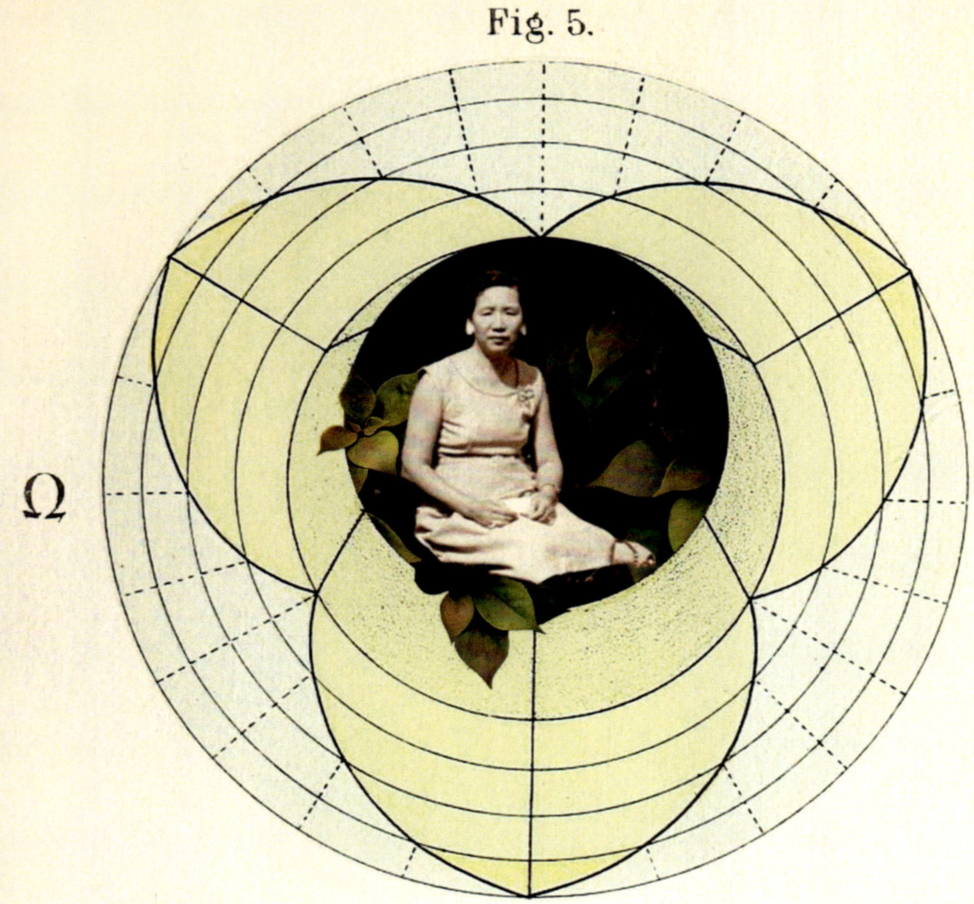

Your mother's mother was named for Precious Jade (FIG. 5. 王珍玉). Your father's mother for Healing Jade (FIG. 6. 楊玉治). Between them is my night's long palm stretching from one hour into ten. Pressing your eyes open. Two chalices still hoping to catch stars under a sky heavy with other people's dreams.

Jade insomnia is the jungle river whose unrest swells beneath the sternum, hidden at the bottom of each interrupted breath. Shame's night traffic collides with each of your faults, glistens wet, blinking in the aftermath.

In the sprite moss of this moment, your fingers touch down on the earth. *Mother of witness, please grant me a home beneath these feet*. Poets are selenologists learning to read craters of loss. The graveyard's silence is flooded by mantras wrangling moisture from distant moonrock.

Jade insomnia is your third eye opening, noticing a little too much. Unable to fathom how close I really am. Trees gather at your window upon the start of another letter that may never arrive. It is the color of disillusionment, how you've been chasing green lights all these years.

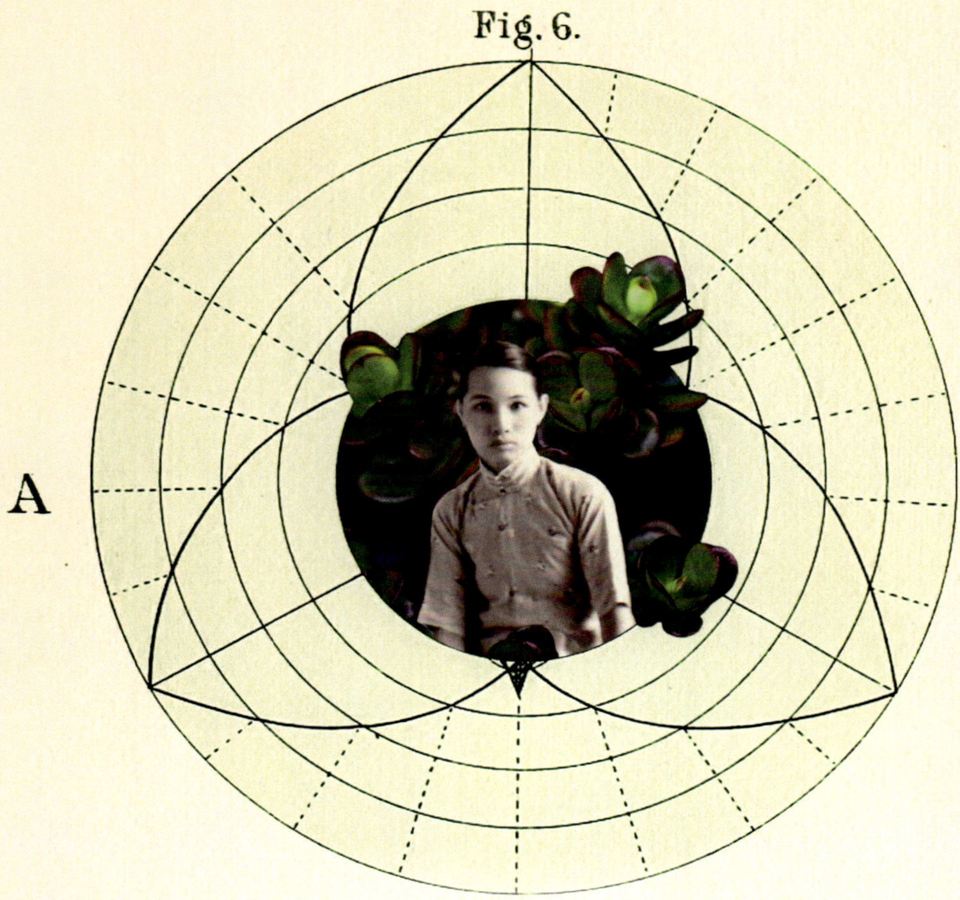

Alone in a deserted office. *You are a bridge to the future of this place*, they say, leaving a dustpan with your name on it, as they push their lifeboats off the littered shore of your spine. They take what they want and leave. What else did you expect?

Jade insomnia is a losing battle. And yet you decide to stay—with me. I watch you glow into luciferin sage, quietly plotting your escape behind doors, in empty stairwells. Try to leave you clues inside envelopes and the lure of kind hazel eyes. I meet you in parking lots, on the page, am waiting outside your overthinking mind, my linden breeze cool against your skin. Sometimes I am an unseen hand bending the light a little closer to you.

Once I came as a stranger into the gallery and when we saw each other, we cried. These days I am fashioning myself a soft baritone voice to whisper your name into all the right ears. Unlike Yunü, I don't walk your dreams in elegant veils, make miracles, or even care to save you. Because here's the thing: You already do it so well on your own.

Remember the difference between the jade of your lineage and the kind that turns me away. Tell me you'll come for me. I admit that I am slow, but definitely worth the fight.

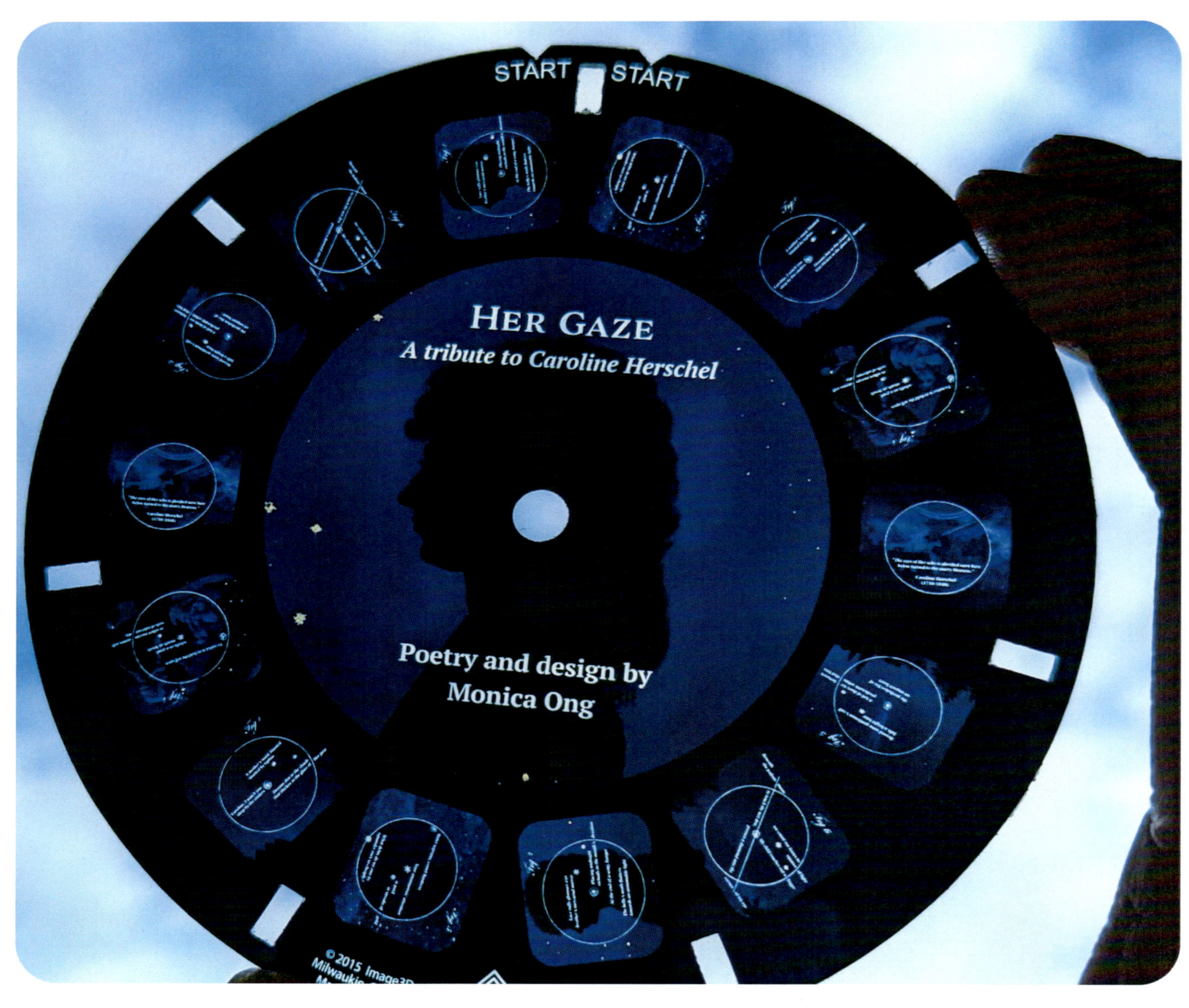

This tribute to Caroline Herschel (1750–1848) is framed by Herschel's sketches of Comet C-1786 P1, which she observed on August 1, 1786, between the constellations Ursa Major and Coma Berenices.

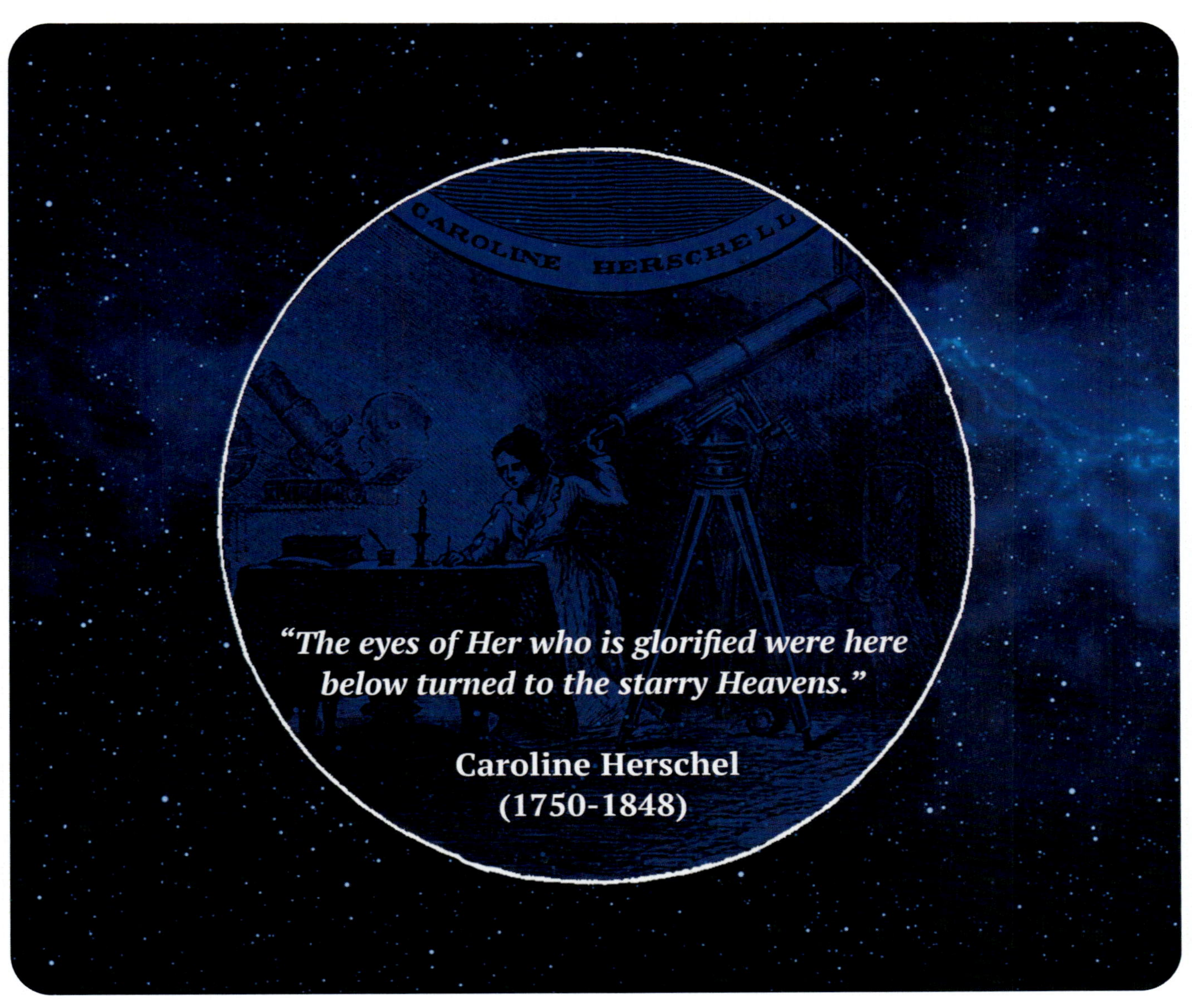
CAROLINE HERSCHEL
"The eyes of Her who is glorified were here below turned to the starry Heavens."
Caroline Herschel
(1750-1848)

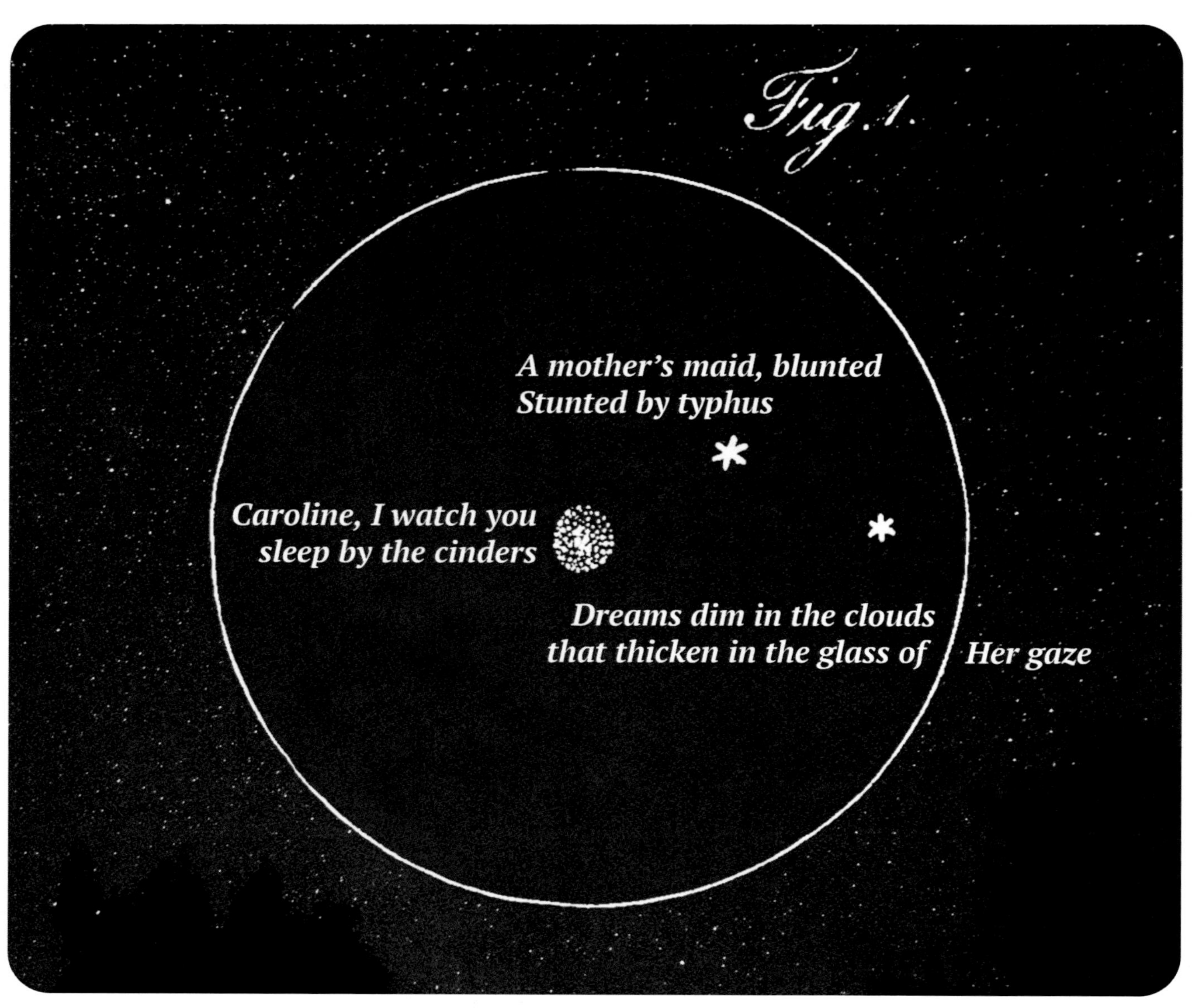
Fig. 1.
A mother's maid, blunted
Stunted by typhus
Caroline, I watch you
sleep by the cinders
Dreams dim in the clouds
that thicken in the glass of
Her gaze

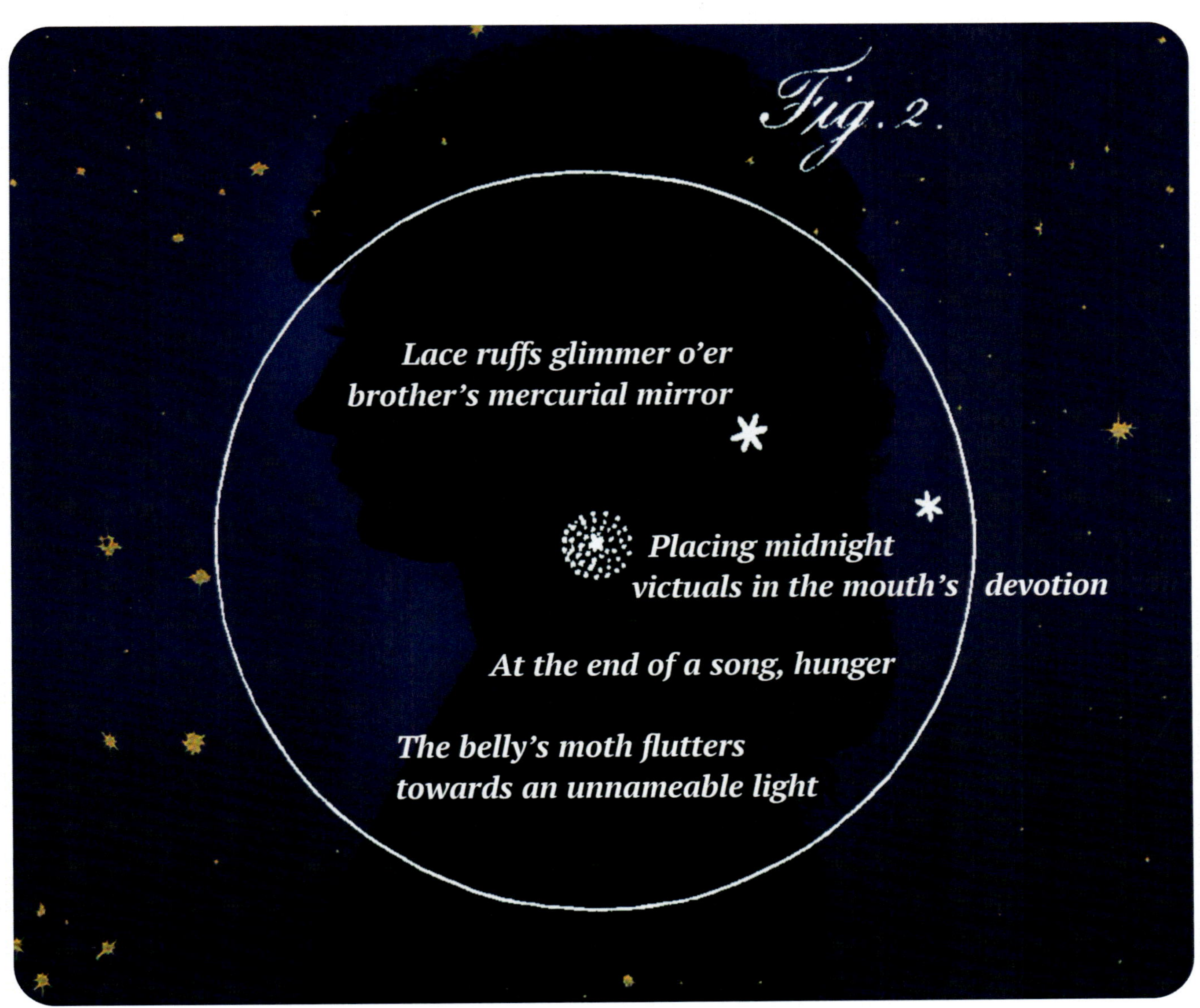
Fig. 2.
Lace ruffs glimmer o'er
brother's mercurial mirror
Placing midnight
victuals in the mouth's devotion
At the end of a song, hunger
The belly's moth flutters
towards an unnameable light

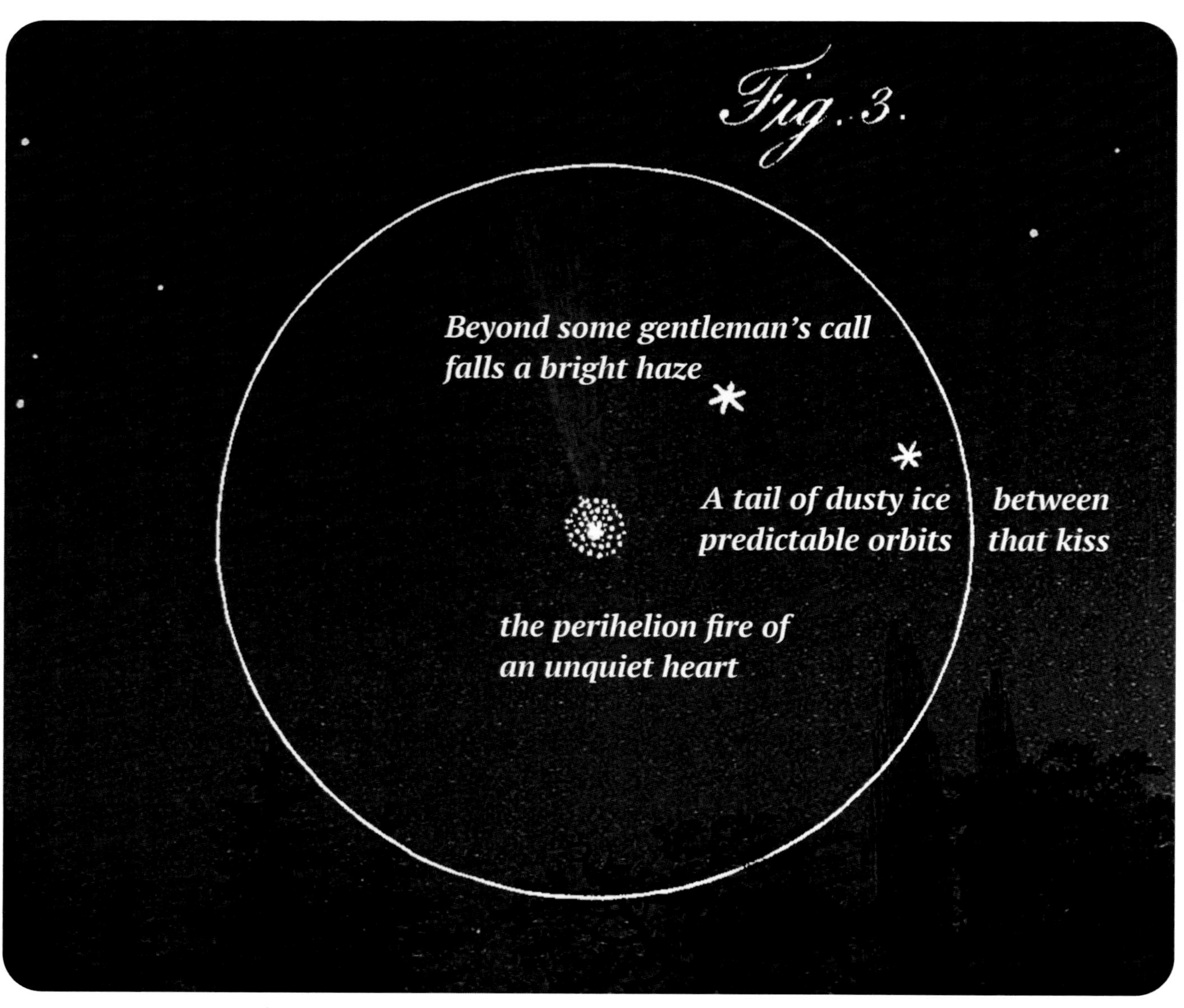
Fig. 3.
Beyond some gentleman's call
falls a bright haze
A tail of dusty ice
predictable orbits
between
that kiss
the perihelion fire of
an unquiet heart

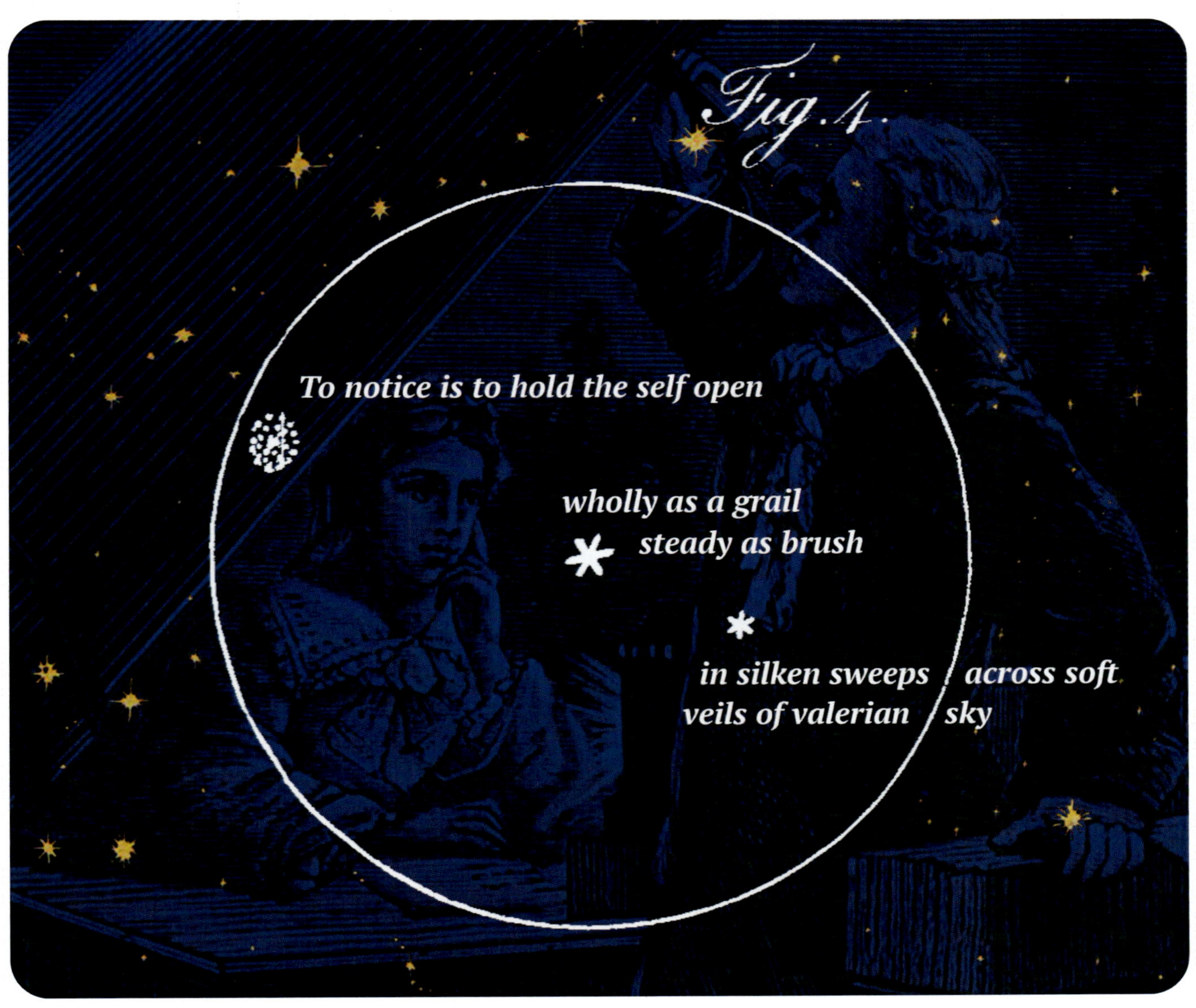
Fig. 4.
To notice is to hold the self open
wholly as a grail
steady as brush
in silken sweeps / across soft
veils of valerian / sky

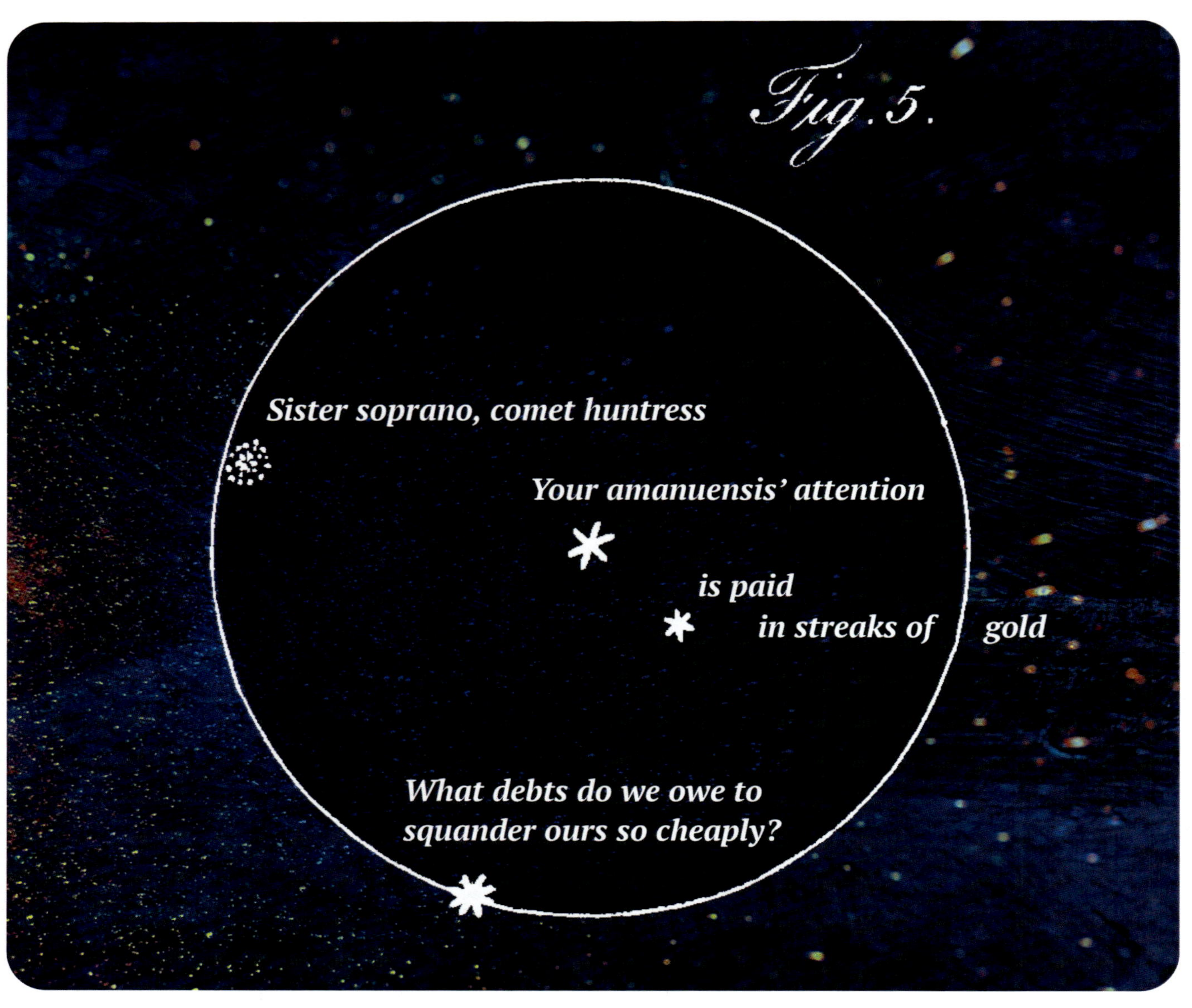
Fig. 5.
Sister soprano, comet huntress
Your amanuensis' attention
is paid
in streaks of gold
What debts do we owe to
squander ours so cheaply?

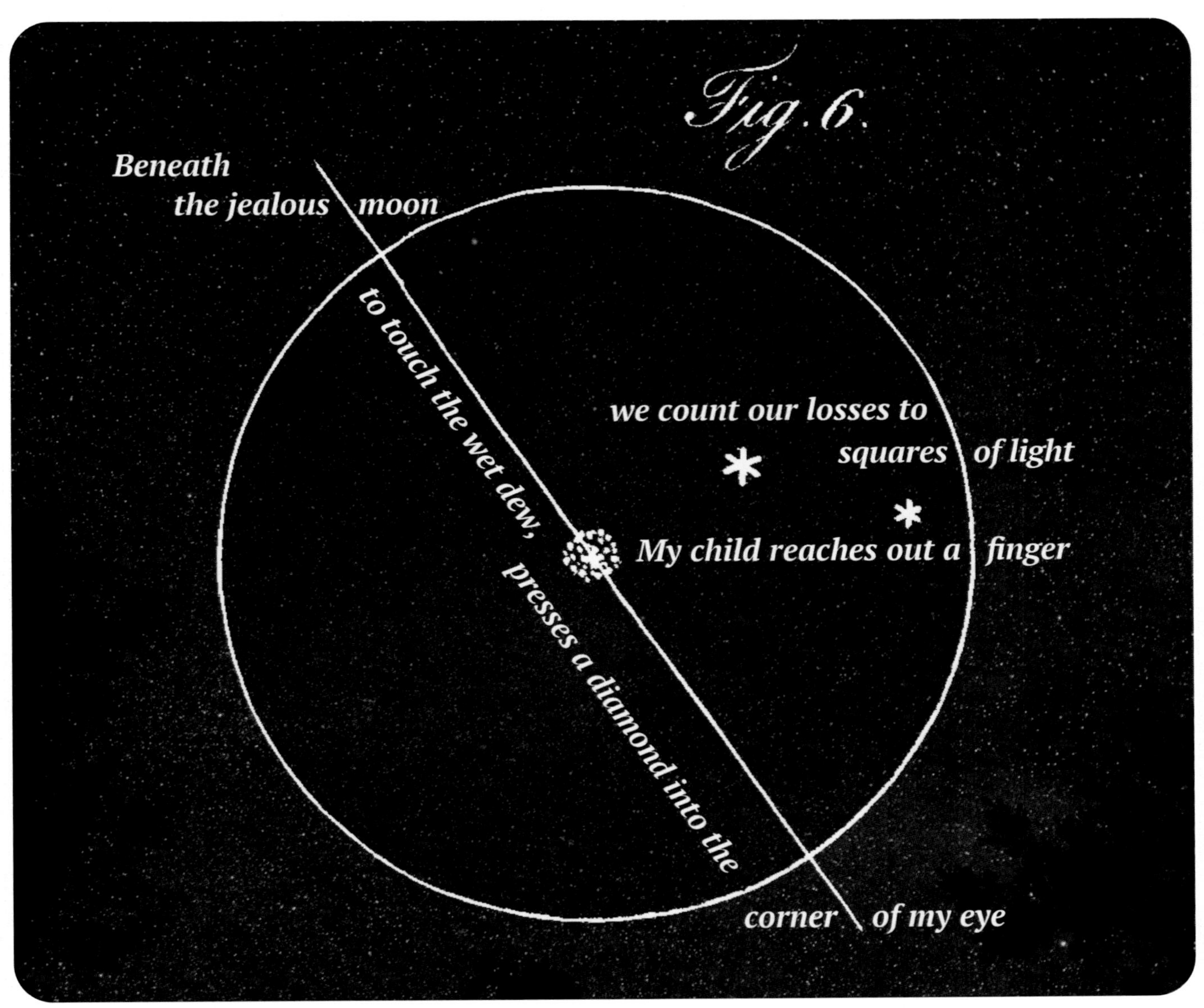
Fig. 6.
Beneath
the jealous moon
to touch the wet dew,
presses a diamond into the
we count our losses to
squares of light
My child reaches out a finger
corner of my eye

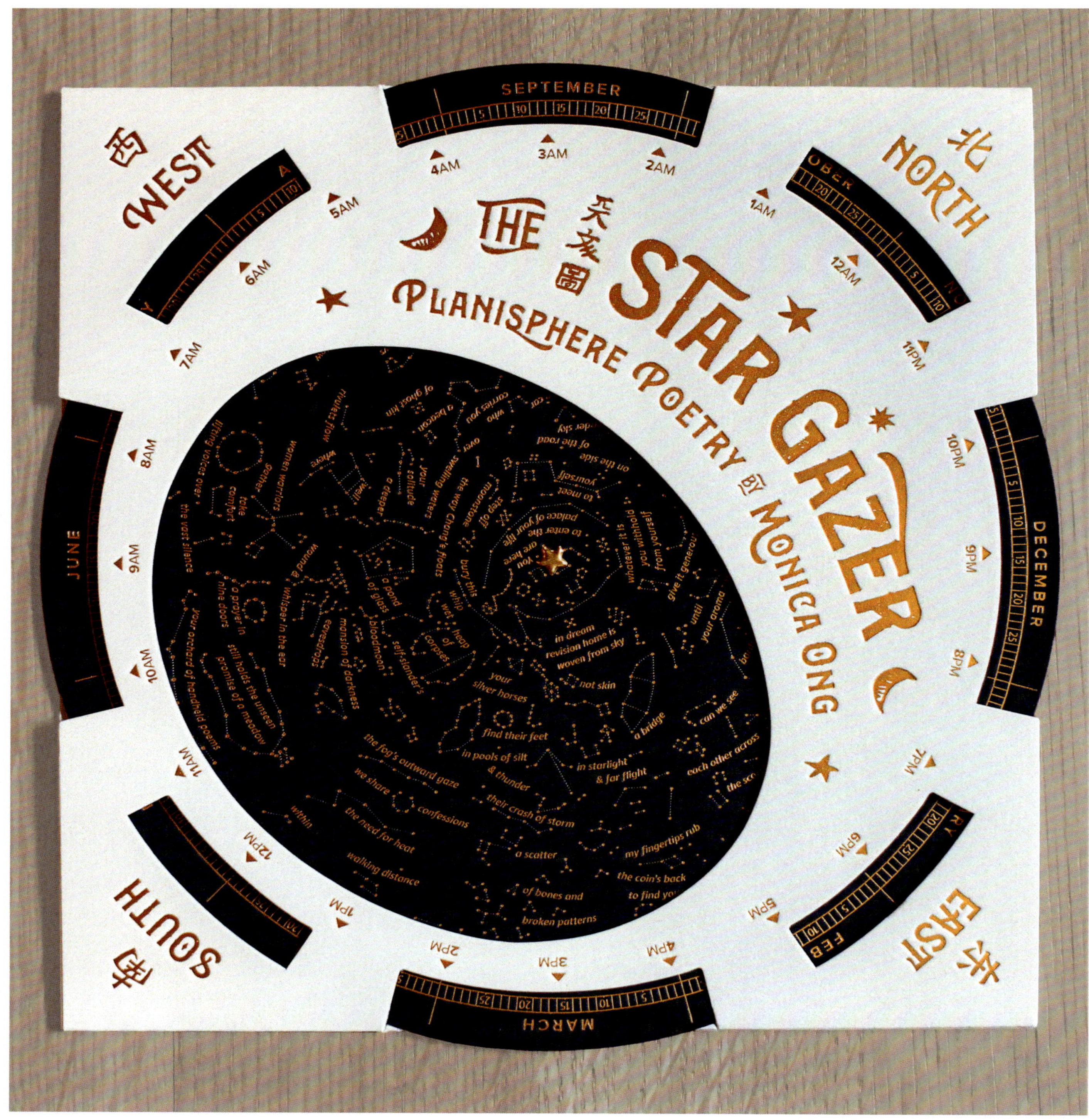

Based on the Soochow Astronomical Chart, c. 1193, this planisphere depicts the Chinese night sky as seen from the northern hemisphere, reflecting a unique poem depending on the alignment of the day and hour.

THE STAR GAZER

You are here
to enter the
palace of your life
to meet yourself
on the side of the road
arms waving
beneath a tender sky

Don't scold
don't fall in the grass
face down, this body
counted among us

Slow the car to a purr
doors unlock from the terrace
secret sails drifting towards
the wing of the red bird

Time's curtain draws open
a temple of incense
my heart in ashes

Step off moonstone
the way Chang'e floats
over swelling waters
who carries you a beacon
of ghost kin

Your solitude, a deeper well
where rivulets flow
willows tap the kitchen window
stars send arrows to
the land of god and soil
Women warriors gather
take comfort
lifting voices over
the vast silence

Bury this whip wet
heap of corpses
a pond of glass
self-slander's bloodmoon
mansion of darkness eavesdrops
wound & whisper in the ear

A prayer in nine doors
still holds the unseen promise
of a meadow
your orchard of handheld poems

Your silver horses find their feet
in pools of silt
the fog's outward gaze
we share
In dream revision home is
woven from sky not skin

Whatever it is
you withhold from yourself
give it generously

** One possible reading of the night sky on March 4, the birthday of Theresa Hak Kyung Cha*

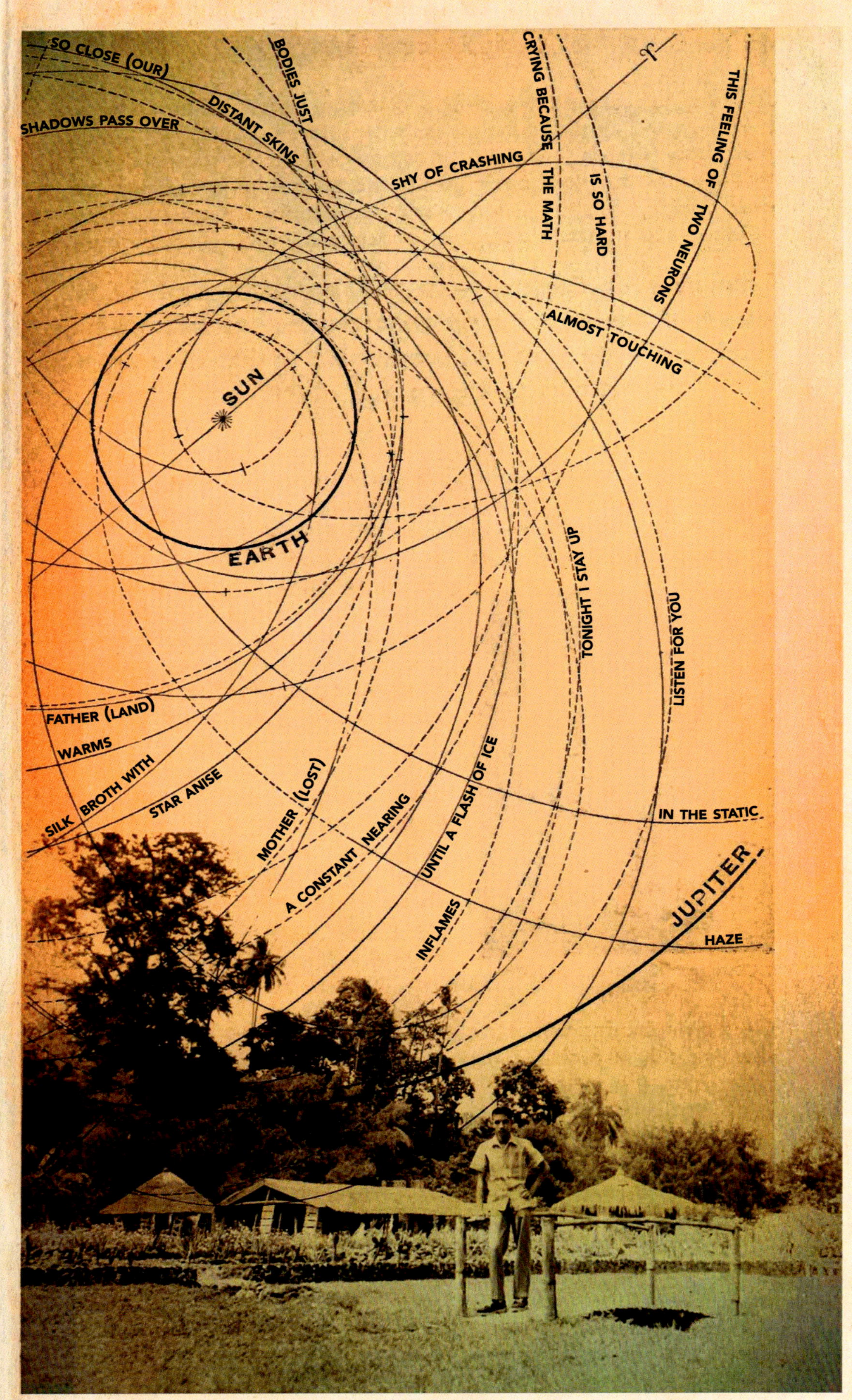

Jupiter's Family of Comets.

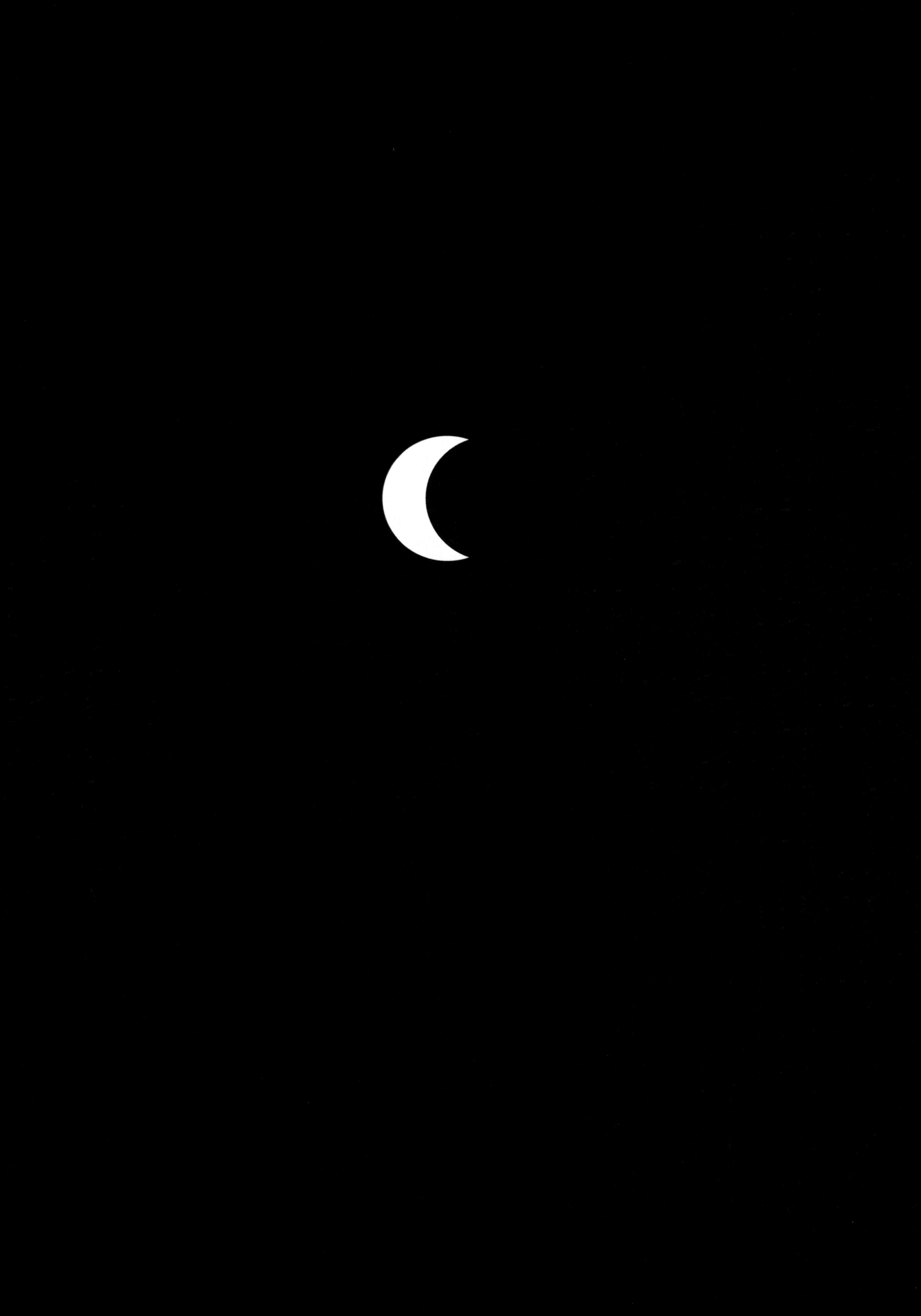

YELLOW INSOMNIA

All sentient beings have at one time been your mother. —Buddhist proverb

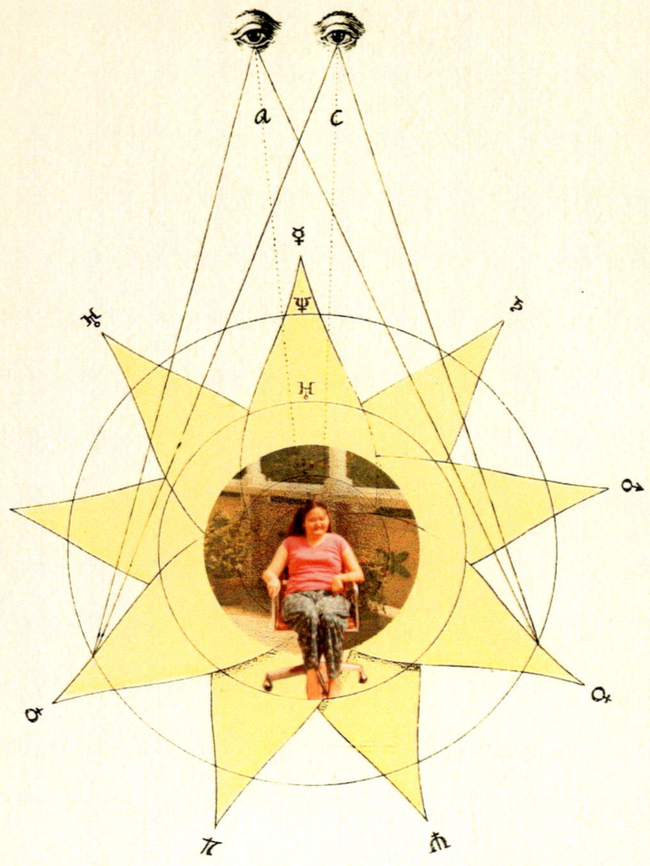

Fig. 19.

Yellow insomnia is the hiss of midnight over another city in flames, a white knee on the black throat of a father shattered, who was, in another life, my father, your father, your father's father, this heart (of our country) ground into the ground. Our shared hurt a constant waking. It is the inability to zoom out and distinguish the wound from the body, the body from the wound. Yellow insomnia is the knowing of being watched by eyes that never learned to see us whole. Walking in skin singed by a weak man's projection of peril. His monsters and mistresses take on the shape of your face, the movement of your hands, your body a shadow beneath this hallucination of America, slowly dying. How to unmake this deadly gaze? When will our love for you be sharp enough to cut the roots of the venomous vine? What is this life if not to honor yours, your daughter's, your daughter's daughter? Despite the drowse of grief, the night brain swells with uncontrolled blossoms of milk thistle and tansy, my troubled questions dotted with their sprawling lace border of blooming yarrow. The way a broken branch when touching soil manages to press its young green fingers into a new hope. Years before aunt Juanita died, I remember her examining me in grandmother's temple from her metal chair, her eyes searching me in prophecy. *There are two demon daughters standing inside you, one at each shoulder*, she said. Now is a door that refuses to close. The black tiger and the golden lion are terrifying or majestic depending on one's faith.

THE DAUGHTER'S ALMANAC

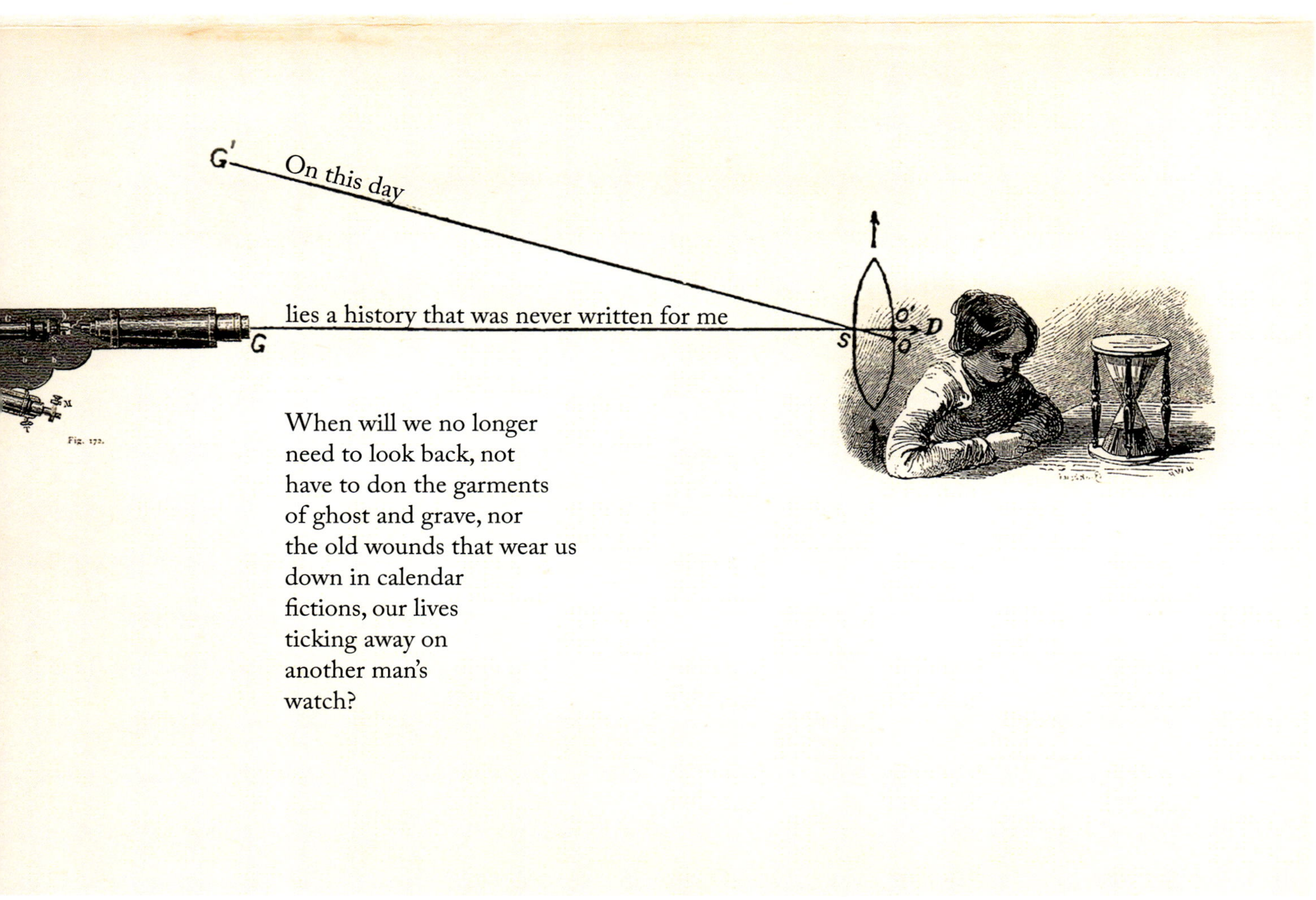

On this day

lies a history that was never written for me

When will we no longer
need to look back, not
have to don the garments
of ghost and grave, nor
the old wounds that wear us
down in calendar
fictions, our lives
ticking away on
another man's
watch?

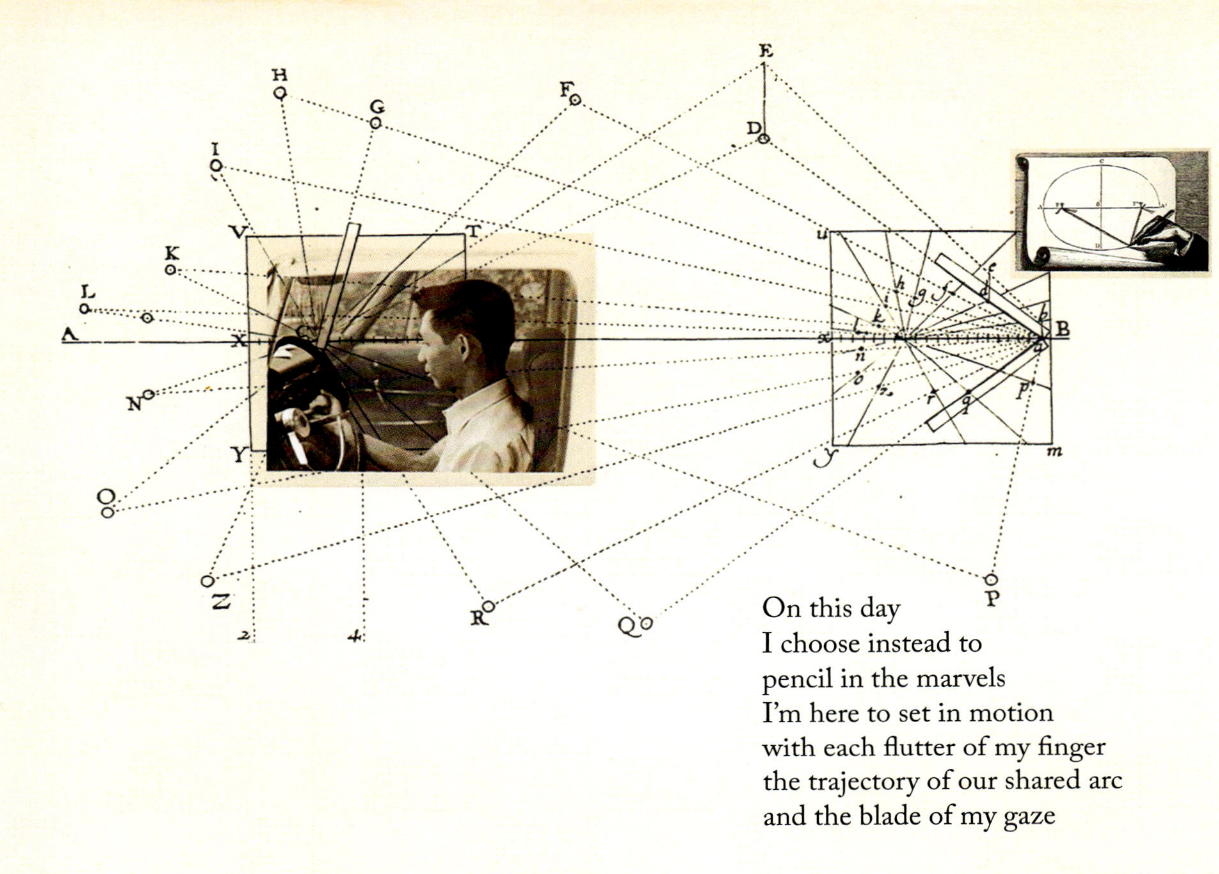

On this day
I choose instead to
pencil in the marvels
I'm here to set in motion
with each flutter of my finger
the trajectory of our shared arc
and the blade of my gaze

my gaze

Perhaps today
these hands will tend the root
of a tree emerging in my
granddaughter's mind as she searches
for me by the river of a new earth
I'll pass along my sun-kissed fruit
and the nectar of rubble-born blooms

tell her, it is *your* tide that calls the moon

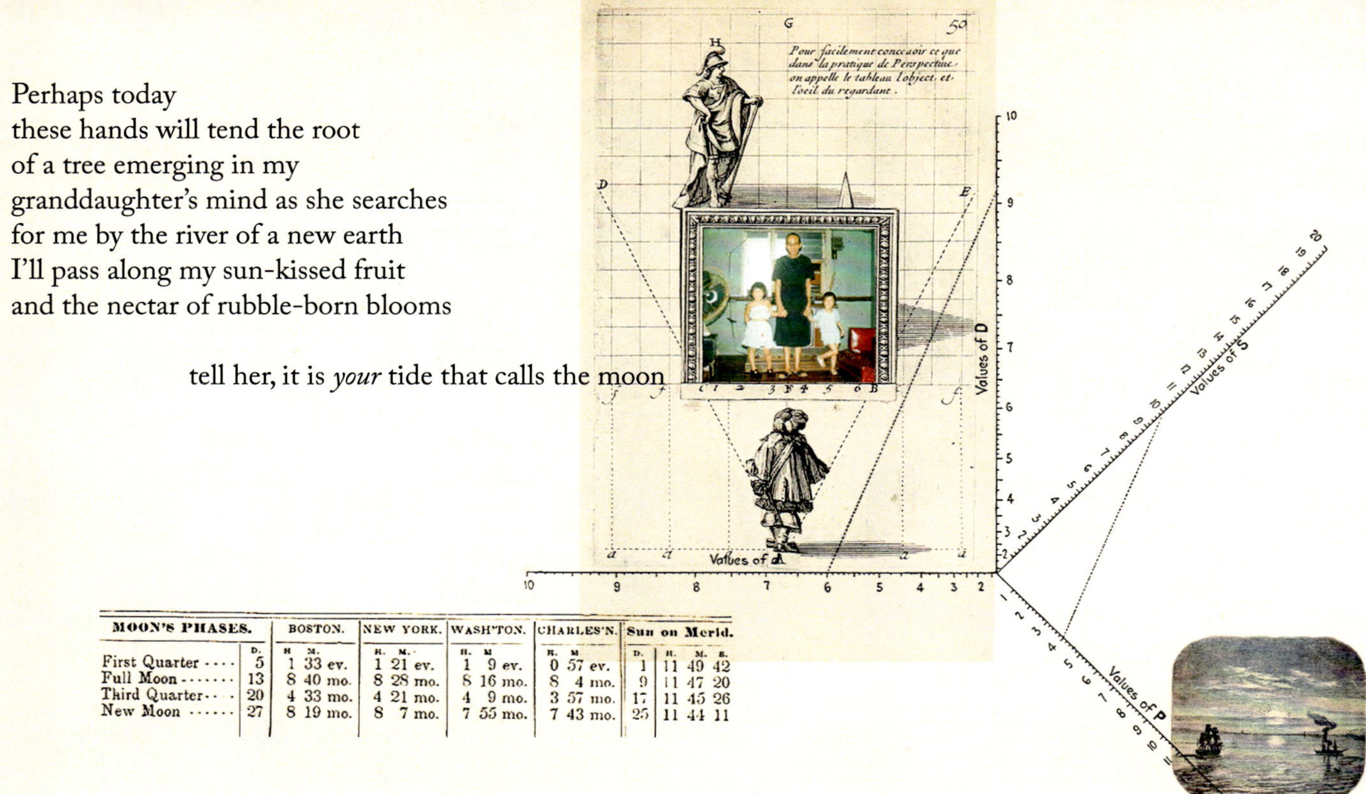

MOON'S PHASES.	D.	BOSTON. H. M.	NEW YORK. H. M.	WASH'TON. H. M.	CHARLES'N. H. M.	Sun on Merid. D.	H. M. S.
First Quarter	5	1 33 ev.	1 21 ev.	1 9 ev.	0 57 ev.	1	11 49 42
Full Moon	13	8 40 mo.	8 28 mo.	8 16 mo.	8 4 mo.	9	11 47 20
Third Quarter...	20	4 33 mo.	4 21 mo.	4 9 mo.	3 57 mo.	17	11 45 26
New Moon	27	8 19 mo.	8 7 mo.	7 55 mo.	7 43 mo.	25	11 44 11

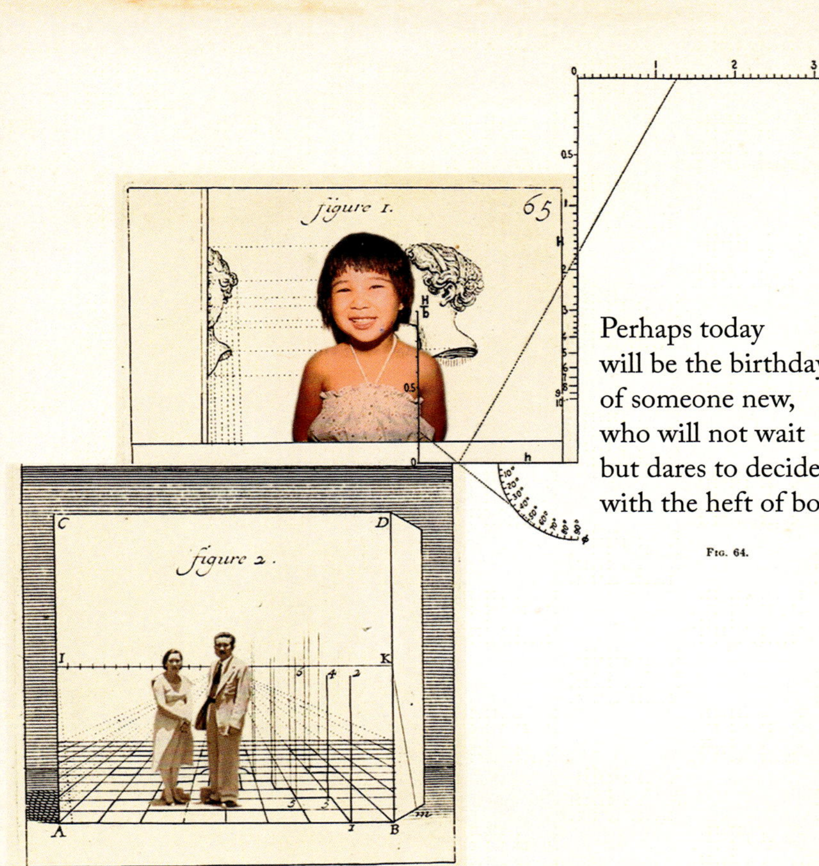

Perhaps today
will be the birthday
of someone new,
who will not wait
but dares to decide
with the heft of both lung and leg

someone who realizes
that the scarecrow is just
deadwood and hay,
that we don't have to be corn or crow
but a story that can move
out of strata across suns
flicking its tail to tip the sky

On this day
I predict that
everything is going to change
I am making invitations
for the homecoming we never had
foiled with stardust
each letter of your name spelled
correctly and hand pressed into velvety kiss cut paper
as though today
were a holy day
curling its lips
beneath your fingers

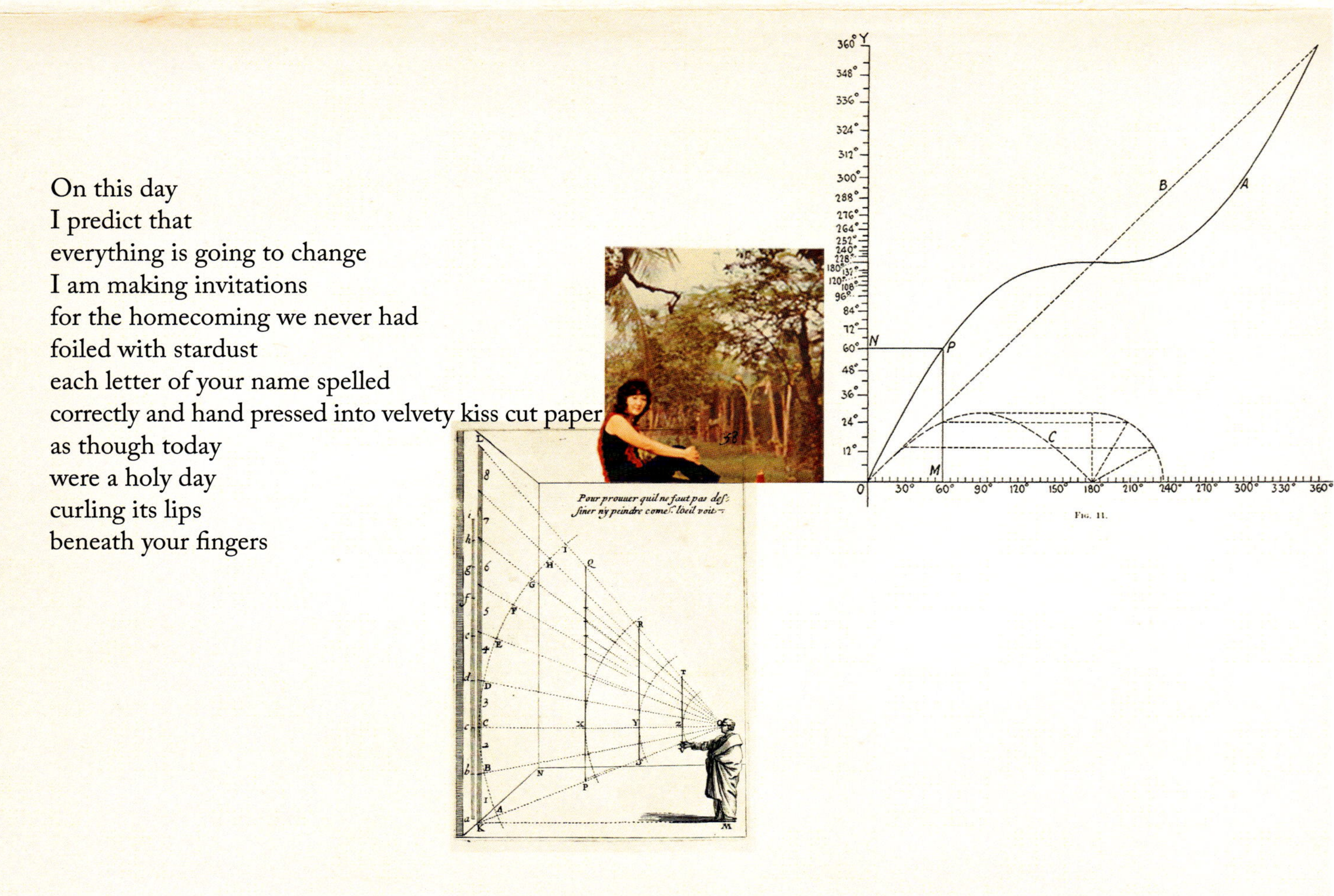

THE DARK SIDE

OF THE MOON

Our labor
rises from
this side
of the moon

EXPLOSIVE
precise
prolific
yet glimpsed
(His)tory's
gaze tidally locked
in libration
on our other half
(not liberation)

Across your ridges
mountains of evidence
map the fission
of your mind
and
the
NOBLE WOMEN
know how to find
each other
in the dark
UNMIRRORED
truth of all things
between motes
of dust
and doubt
Another word
for genius is
Pay no mind
COURAGEOUS
to stares that care
HERO
we did
much more
than
only to caress
survive
the surface

Some of us teach our
DAUGHTERS
In weak
to hang
interactions
among particles or men
red lanterns at the
you proved
ends of their limbs
more than anyone
how symmetry is
wonder where they
VIOLATED
wander in the cold
cobalt night
In your
shadow
my sleep breaks
fields of GLASSWING
BUTTERFLIES
shatter
the myopic
sky

invisible in
plain sight
flying straight
into this eye

Dr. Chien-Shiung Wu (1912–1997) was a Chinese American experimental physicist. In 1956 she was approached by colleagues Tsung-Dao Lee and Chen-Ning Yang to devise experiments to disprove the law of parity conservation in radioactive decay. Wu placed cobalt-60 into an electromagnetic field at low temperatures and observed that weak interactions among particles were not always symmetrical, overturning a long-held principle of physics. Thanks to the Wu experiment, Lee and Yang were awarded the 1957 Nobel Prize in Physics. Wu, however, was not included. Her name Chien-Shiung (健雄) translates as *courageous hero*.

THE DARK SIDE OF THE MOON

Our labor
rises from
this side
of the moon

EXPLOSIVE
precise
prolific
yet glimpsed
in libration
(not liberation)

(His)tory's gaze
tidally locked
on our other half

Across your ridges
mountains of evidence
map the fission
of your mind and the
UNMIRRORED
truth of all things

NOBLE WOMEN
know how to find
each other
in the dark
between motes
of dust
and doubt

Pay no mind
to stares that care
only to caress
the surface

Some of us teach our
DAUGHTERS
to hang
red lanterns at the
ends of their limbs

wonder where they
wander in the cold
cobalt night

In weak interactions
between particles
or men
you proved
more than anyone
how symmetry is
VIOLATED

In your shadow
my sleep breaks
fields of
GLASSWING
BUTTERFLIES
shatter
the myopic
sky

invisible in
plain sight
flying straight
into this eye

Dr. Chien-Shiung Wu (1912–1997) was a Chinese American experimental physicist. In 1956 she was approached by colleagues Tsung-Dao Lee and Chen-Ning Yang to devise experiments to disprove the law of parity conservation in radioactive decay. Wu placed cobalt-60 into an electromagnetic field at low temperatures and observed that weak interactions among particles were not always symmetrical, overturning a long-held principle of physics. Thanks to the Wu experiment, Lee and Yang were awarded the 1957 Nobel Prize in Physics. Wu, however, was not included. Her name Chien-Shiung (健雄) translates as *courageous hero.*

It is I, sea gull

It
is I
d a w n
& w i n g
It is I
dissolving
into We who
refuse to
let each
Other go
Eyes dead
center in
the storm
Eyes open
Eyes not
looking away
Up here the
view is blue
c r y s t a l l i n e
vivid as your
child's breath
upon the face
High above the
low white squall
Our earth's arc
looks back asks
if the eyes can
hold more than
old fictions in
I black and white I
you fire and exile you
with or against On the edge
of the breath's resis tance:
Lift. Life's bodies in bloom
Bright spectra of colors rise
up in trajectories wider than
these tiny histories Your
flight lets them know what they
didn't know someone like you
could do My grandmother lived
in a world she could not read
not realizing that it takes a
lifetime to understand the
language of her hands that my
books have no translation for
hopes battered & boiled in hot
chili oil that while code is
binary our wholeness cannot
be confined to the poverty of
numbers and small talk about
the weather as a means for
safety of staying out of sight
What names do you carry with
you in the slow skyward burn
What forces push up against your
mettle and shine
Today vs. the downward pull
Today vs. another body
into the ground
Today vs. legacy
marred by man's mistakes
To what devotion
do you circle with the lens of each year
Who do you tend to with the pine air passing
from the night's ghost lung?
through the day lung
What
do you release
without regret
Our maps
blood drawn point us
far beyond the orange haze
of sun-collapsed empires
Daughter diaspora Son of samaya
This is your time To b e
s e e n

t o b e s e e n
t o b e s e e n
t o b e s e e n

SEAGULL

"It is I, Seagull." –Valentina Tereshkova, first woman in space.

It is I, Seagull
It is I, dawn and wing

It is I, dissolving into We
who refuse to let each other go

Eyes dead center in the storm
Eyes open

Eyes not looking away
Up here the view is blue crystalline

vivid as your child's breath upon the face
High above the low white squall

Our earth's arc looks back
asks if the eyes can hold more

than old fictions in
I / black and white / I

you / fire and exile / you
with or against

On the edge
of the breath's resistance: Lift.

Life's bodies in bloom
Bright spectra of colors

rise up in trajectories wider than
these tiny histories

Your flight lets them know
what they didn't know

someone like you could do
My grandmother lived

in a world she could not read
not realizing that it takes

a lifetime to understand
the language of her hands

that my books have no translation for
hopes battered & boiled in hot chili oil

that while code is binary
our wholeness cannot be

confined to the poverty of numbers
and small talk about the weather

as a means for safety
of staying out of sight

What names do you carry with you
in the slow skyward burn

What forces push up against
your mettle and shine

Today vs. the downward pull
Today vs. another body into the ground

Today vs. legacy marred
by man's mistakes

To what devotion do you circle
with the lens of each year

Who do you tend to with the pine air
passing through the day lung

What do you release without regret
from the night's ghost lung?

Our maps blood drawn
point us far beyond the orange haze

of sun-collapsed empires
Daughter diaspora

Son of samaya
This is your time

to be seen
to be seen

to be seen
to be seen

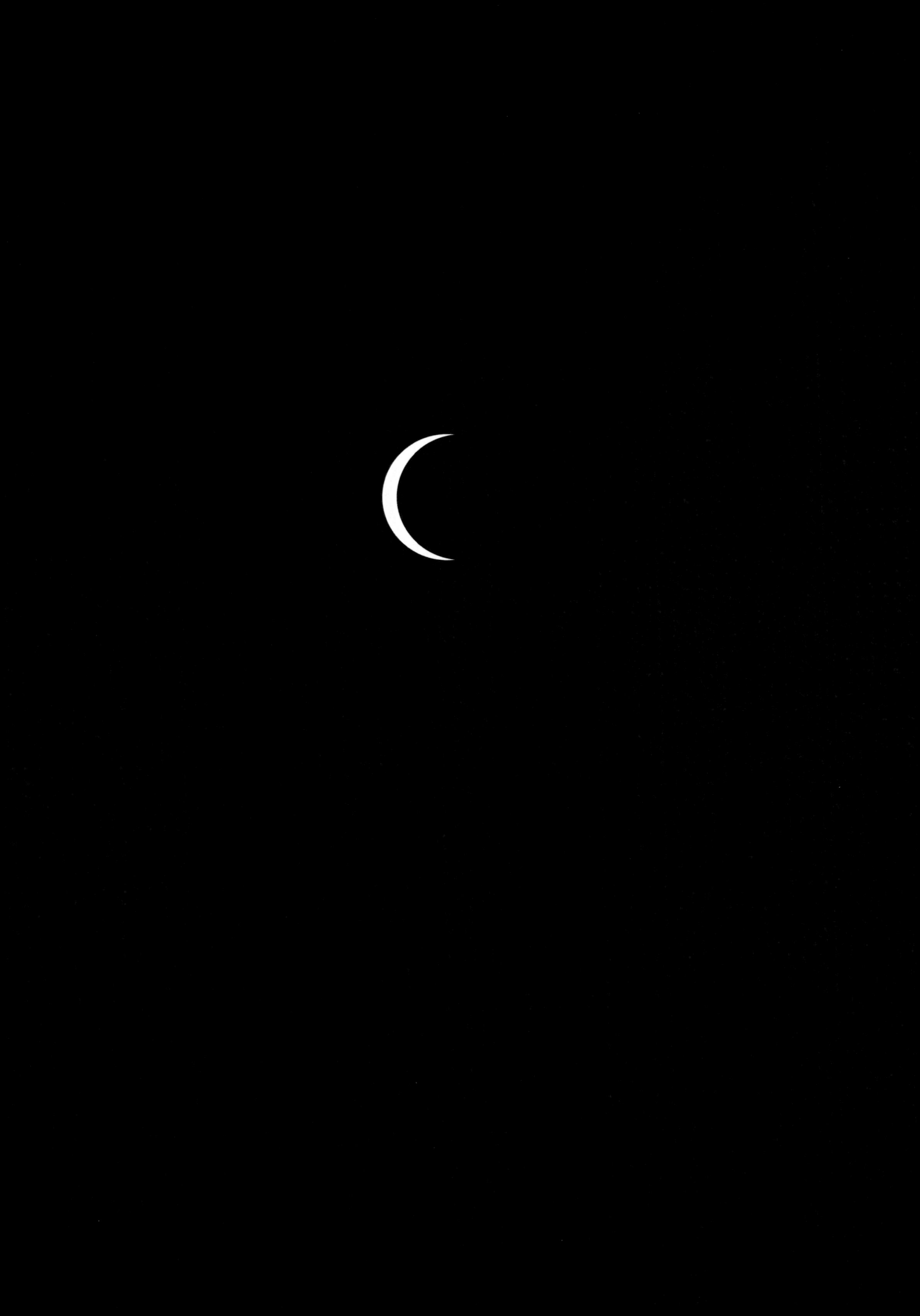

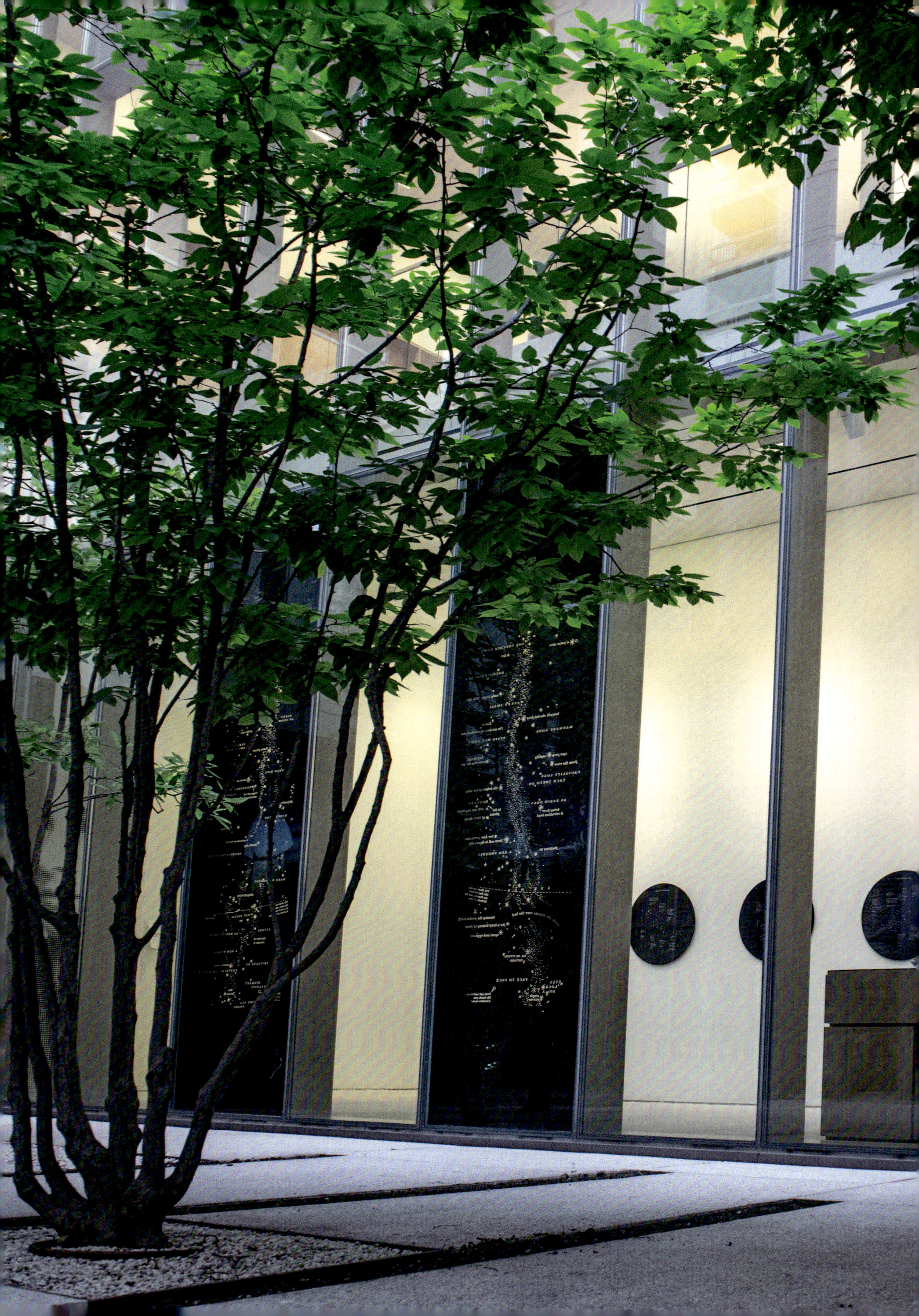

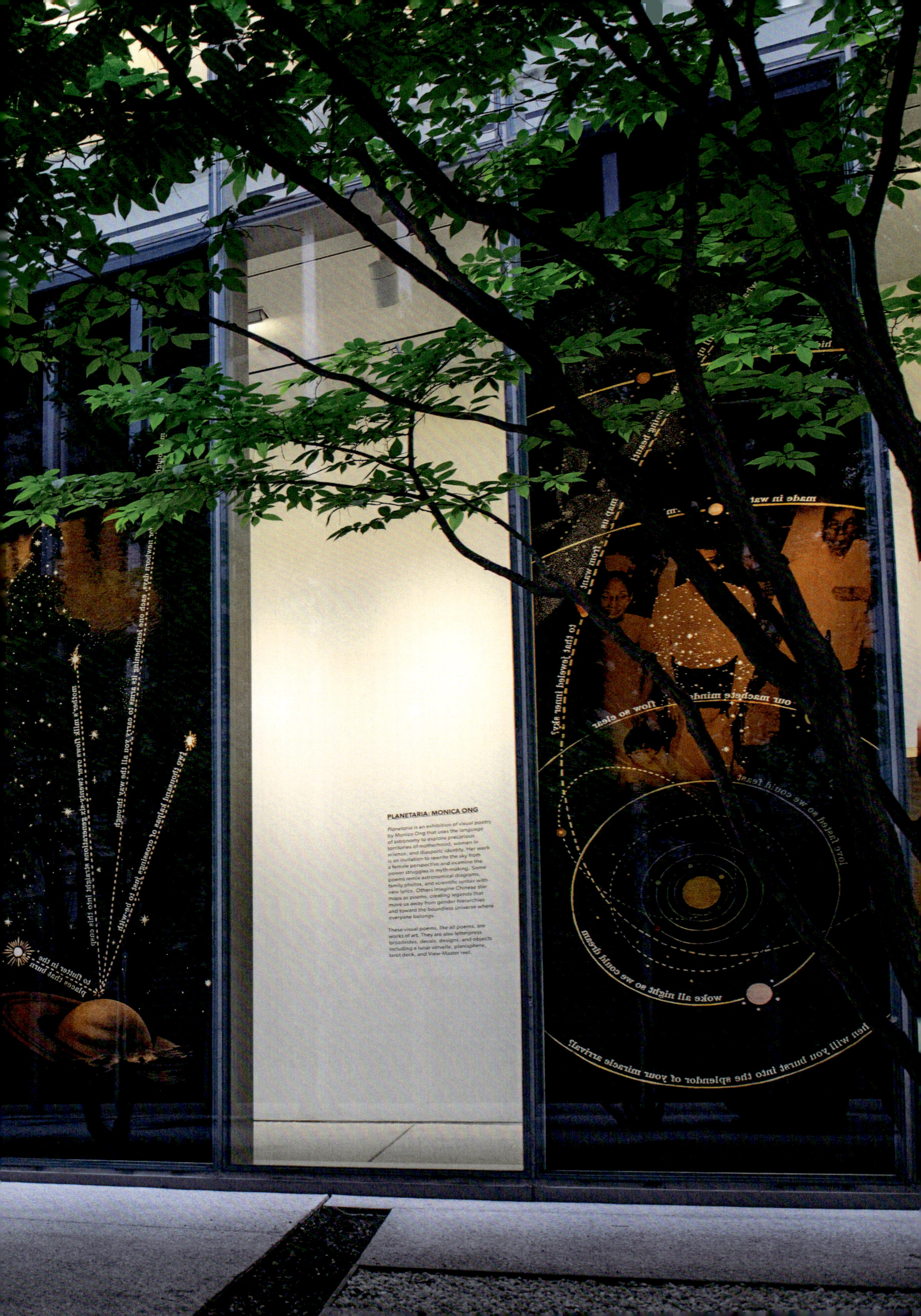
PLANETARIA: MONICA ONG
Planetaria is an exhibition of visual poetry by Monica Ong that uses the language of astronomy to explore precarious territories of motherhood, women in science, and diasporic identity. Her work is an invitation to rewrite the sky from a female perspective and examine the power struggles in myth-making. Some poems remix astronomical diagrams, family photos, and scientific syntax with new lyrics. Others imagine Chinese star maps as poems, creating legends that move us away from gender hierarchies and toward the boundless universe where everyone belongs.
These visual poems, like all poems, are works of art. They are also letterpress broadsides, decals, designs, and objects including a lunar volvelle, planisphere, tarot deck, and View-Master reel.
our machete minds
flow so clear
woke all night so we could dream

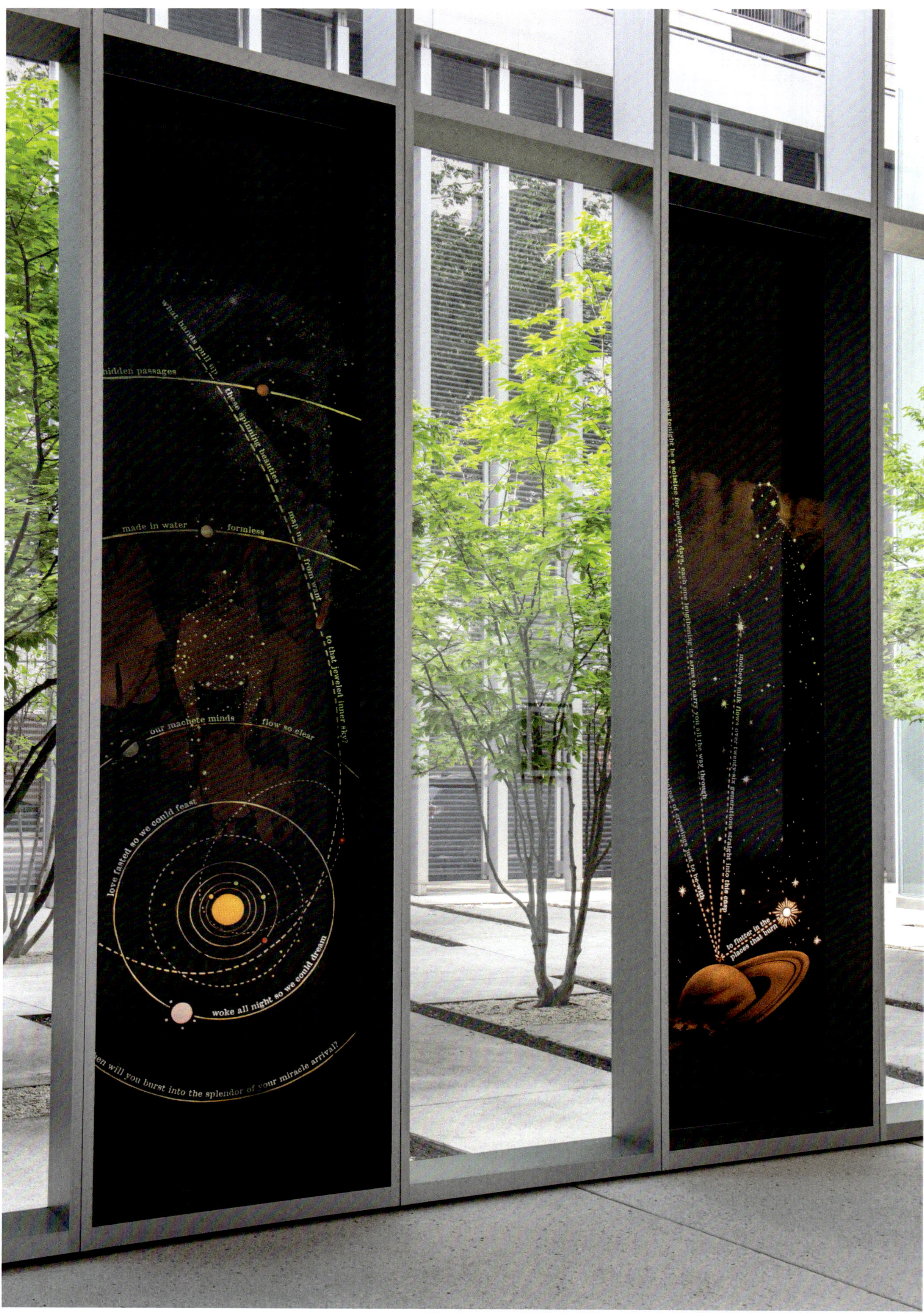
what hands pull up
these spinning beauties
map us
from want
to that jeweled inner sky?
passages
made in water
formless
our machete minds
flow so clear
love fasted so we could feast
woke all night so we could dream
will you burst into the splendor of your miracle arrival?
be a solstice for newborn days, each one lengthening its arms to carry you all the way through
mother's milk flows over twenty-six generations straight into this
of crossings just to be with
to flutter in the
places that burn

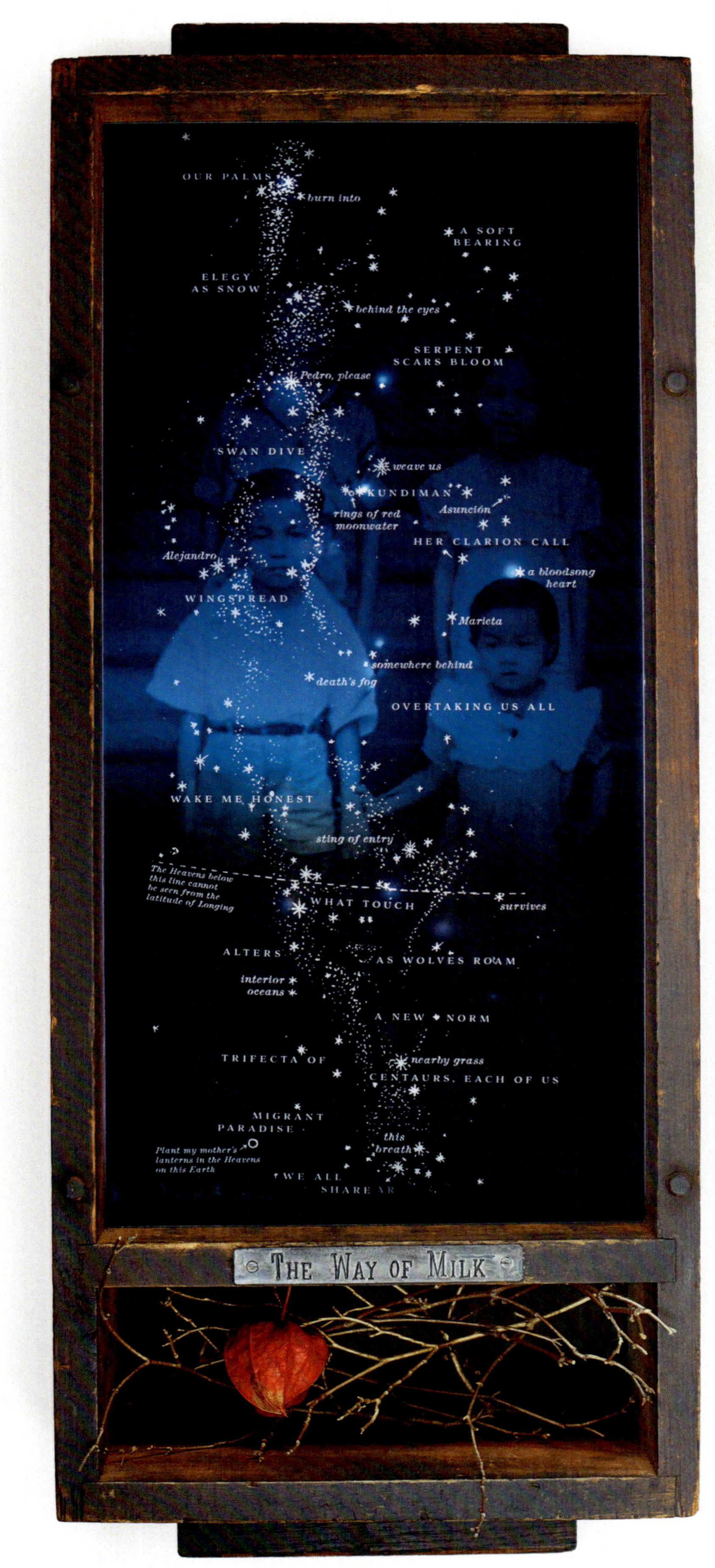
OUR PALMS
burn into
A SOFT BEARING
ELEGY AS SNOW
behind the eyes
SERPENT SCARS BLOOM
Pedro, please
SWAN DIVE
weave us
KUNDIMAN
Asunción
rings of red moonwater
HER CLARION CALL
Alejandro
a bloodsong heart
WINGSPREAD
Marieta
somewhere behind
death's fog
OVERTAKING US ALL
WAKE ME HONEST
sting of entry
The Heavens below this line cannot be seen from the latitude of Longing
WHAT TOUCH
survives
ALTERS
AS WOLVES ROAM
interior oceans
A NEW NORM
TRIFECTA OF
nearby grass
CENTAURS, EACH OF US
MIGRANT PARADISE
Plant my mother's lanterns in the Heavens on this Earth
this breath
WE ALL
SHARE
THE WAY OF MILK

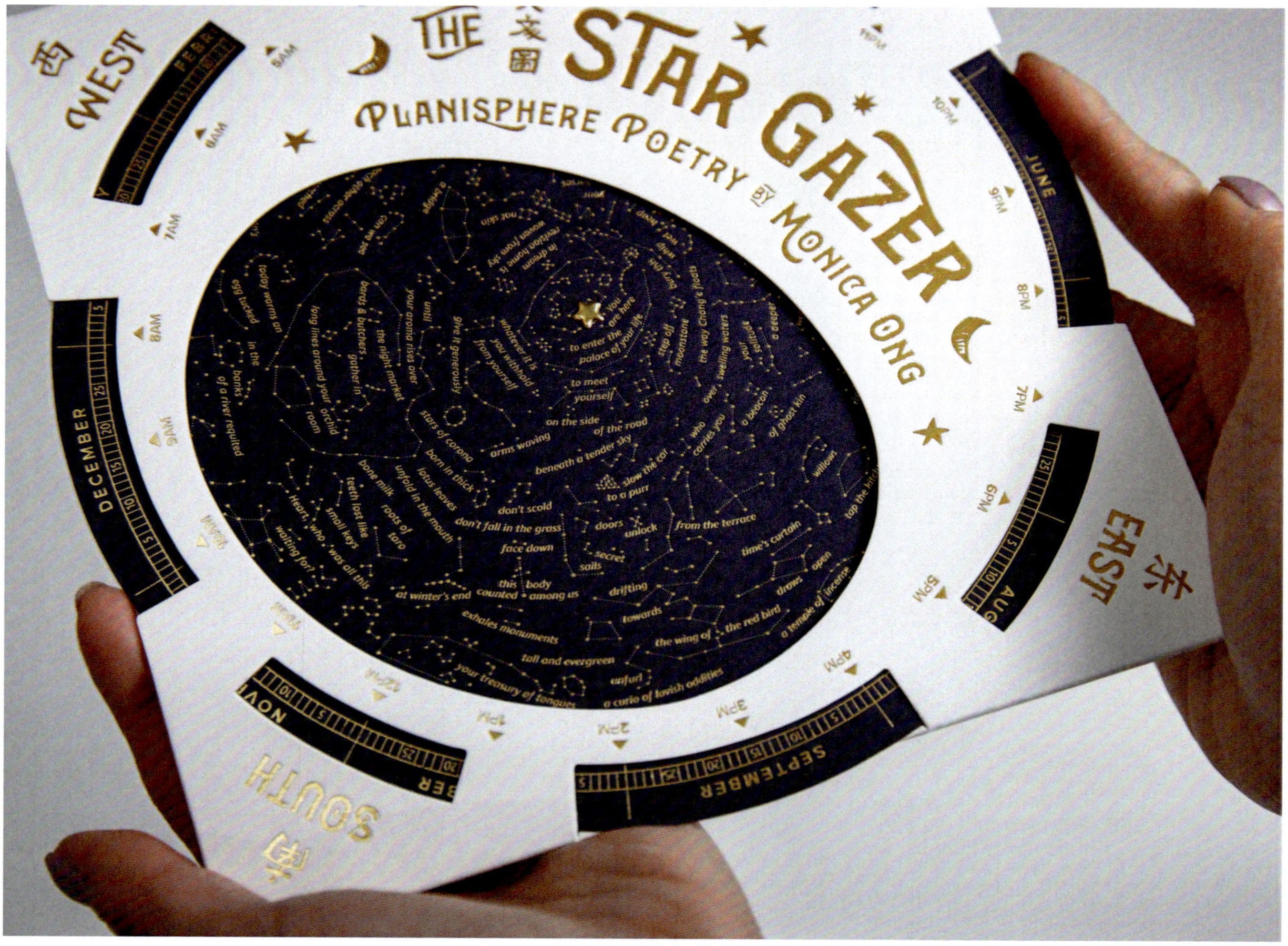
THE STAR GAZER
PLANISPHERE POETRY BY MONICA ONG
WEST
EAST
SOUTH
DECEMBER
SEPTEMBER
JUNE
You are here
to enter the palace of your life
to meet yourself
on the side of the road
beneath a tender sky
arms waving
stars of corona
born in thick lotus leaves
unfold in the mouth
bone milk
roots of taro
don't scold
don't fall in the grass
slow the car to a purr
doors unlock
from the terrace
time's curtain
face down
secret sails
drifting
towards
the wing of the red bird
this body counted among us
at winter's end
exhales monuments
tall and evergreen
your treasury of tongues
unfurl
a curio of lavish oddities

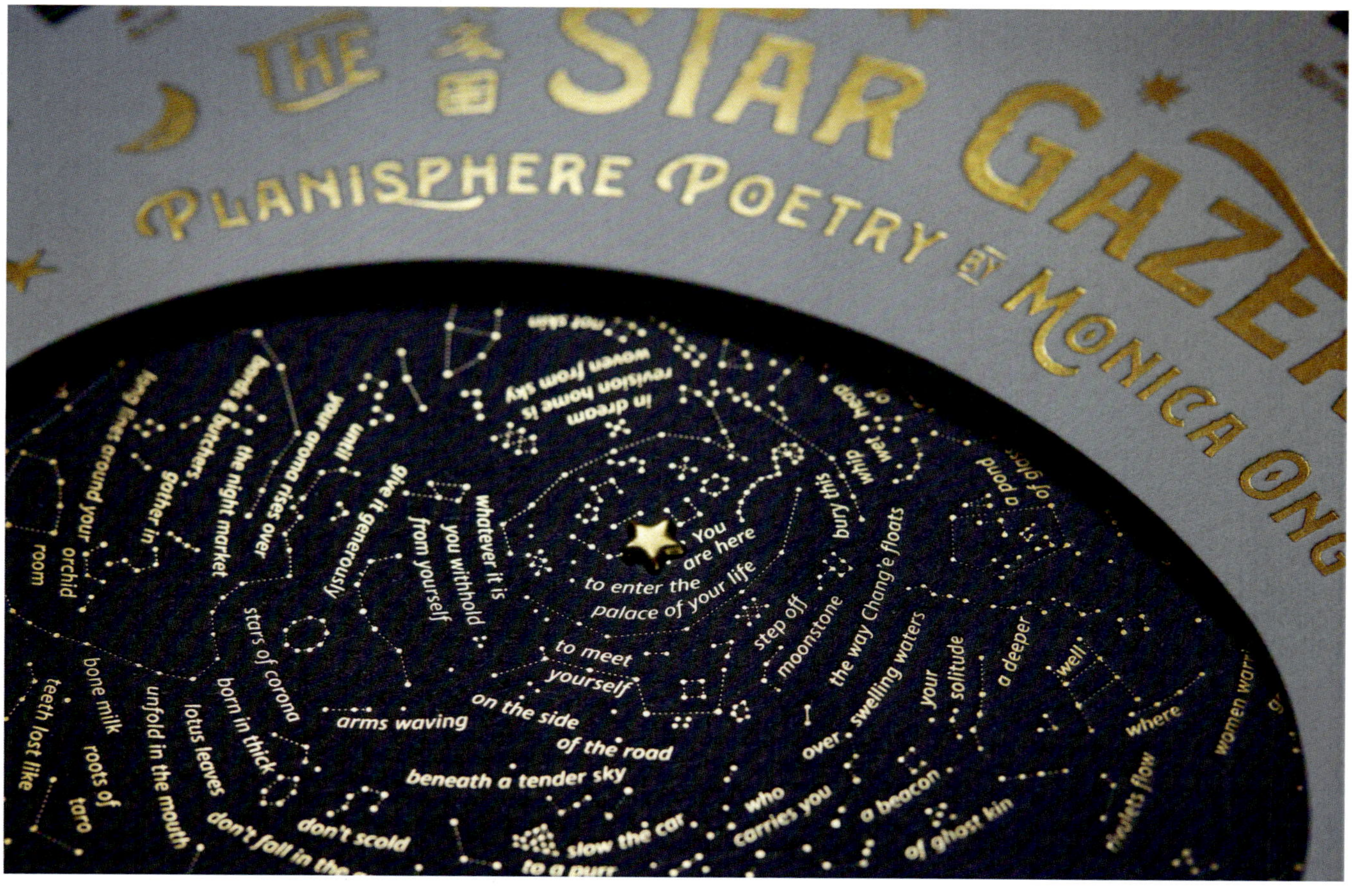
THE STAR GAZER
PLANISPHERE POETRY BY MONICA ONG
in dream
revision home is
woven from sky
until
your aroma rises over
the night market
bards & butchers
gather in
long lines around your
orchid
room
give it generously
whatever it is
you withhold
from yourself
You are here
to enter the
palace of your life
to meet
yourself
step off
moonstone
the way Chang'e floats
over swelling waters
your solitude
a deeper well
bury this
stars of corona
born in thick
lotus leaves
unfold in the mouth
bone milk
roots of
taro
teeth lost like
arms waving
on the side
of the road
beneath a tender sky
who carries you
a beacon
of ghost kin
where
violets flow
don't scold
slow the car
to a purr

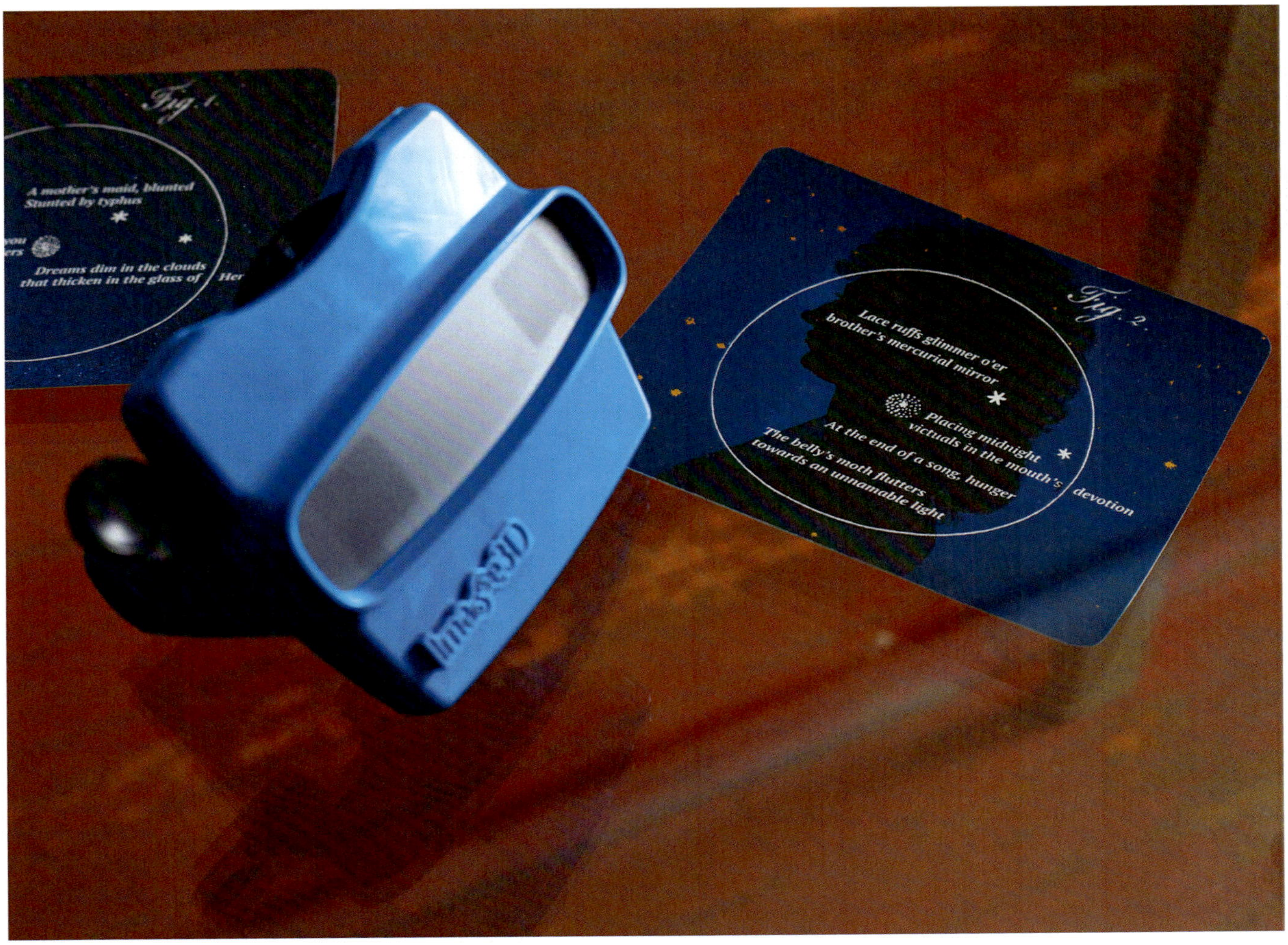

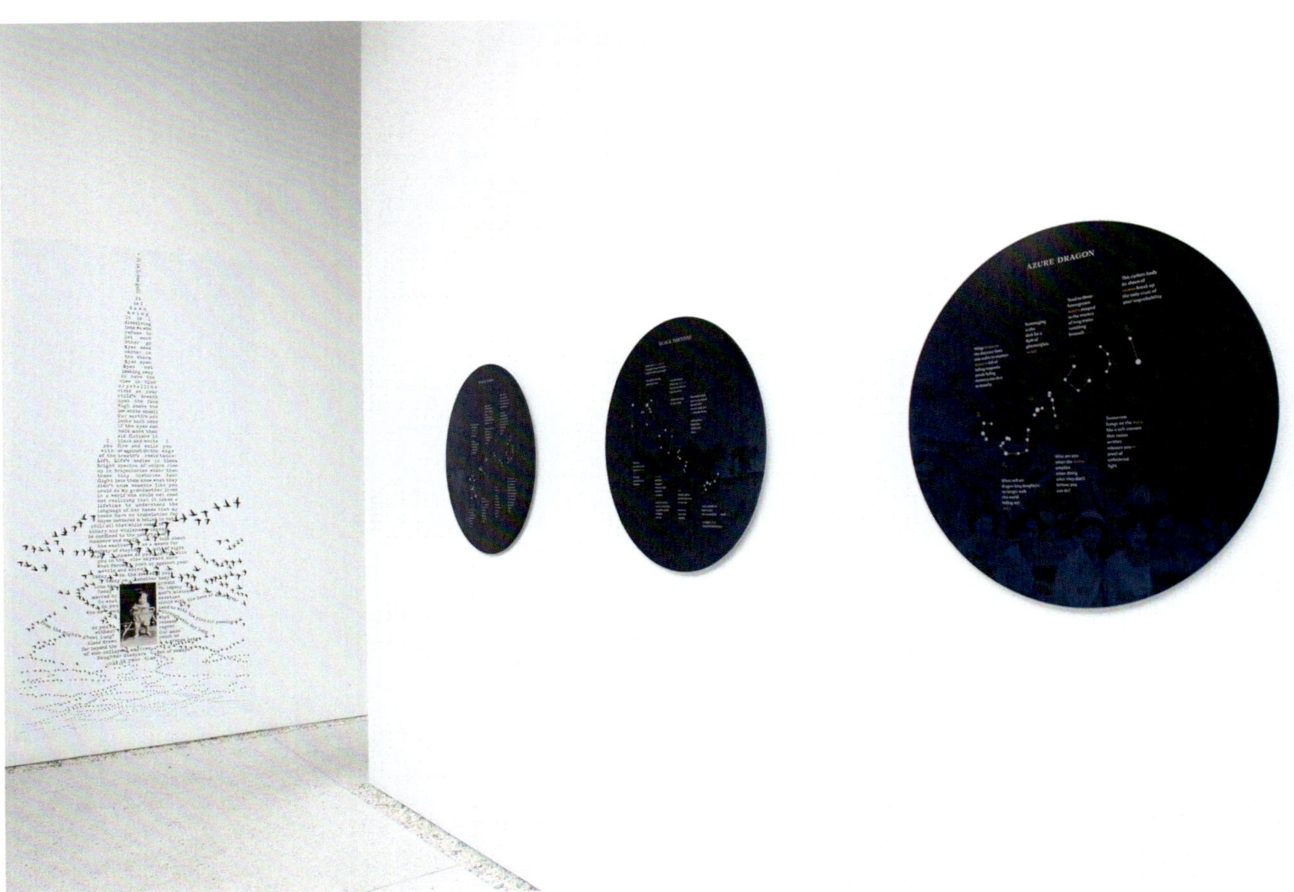
AZURE DRAGON

PURPLE FORBIDDEN ENCLOSURE

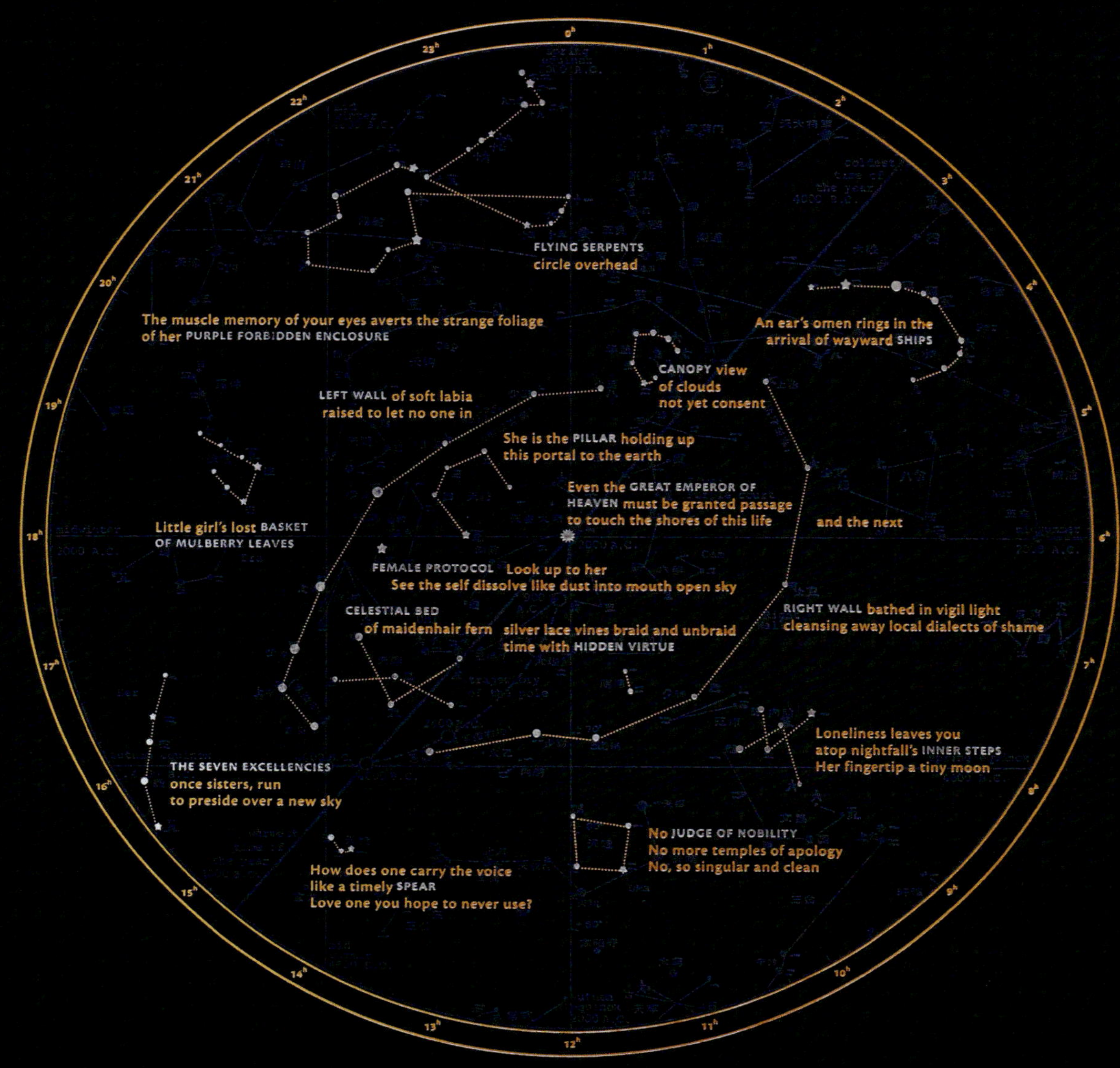

Upper sector of the Northern hemisphere, +40° to +90° declination with selected constellations both inside and outside the walls of the Purple Forbidden Enclosure (紫微垣). Positioned on a celestial north pole, this central court outranks all other courts, its rule of power spread out like a mother's worry from wall to wall, sky to sky.

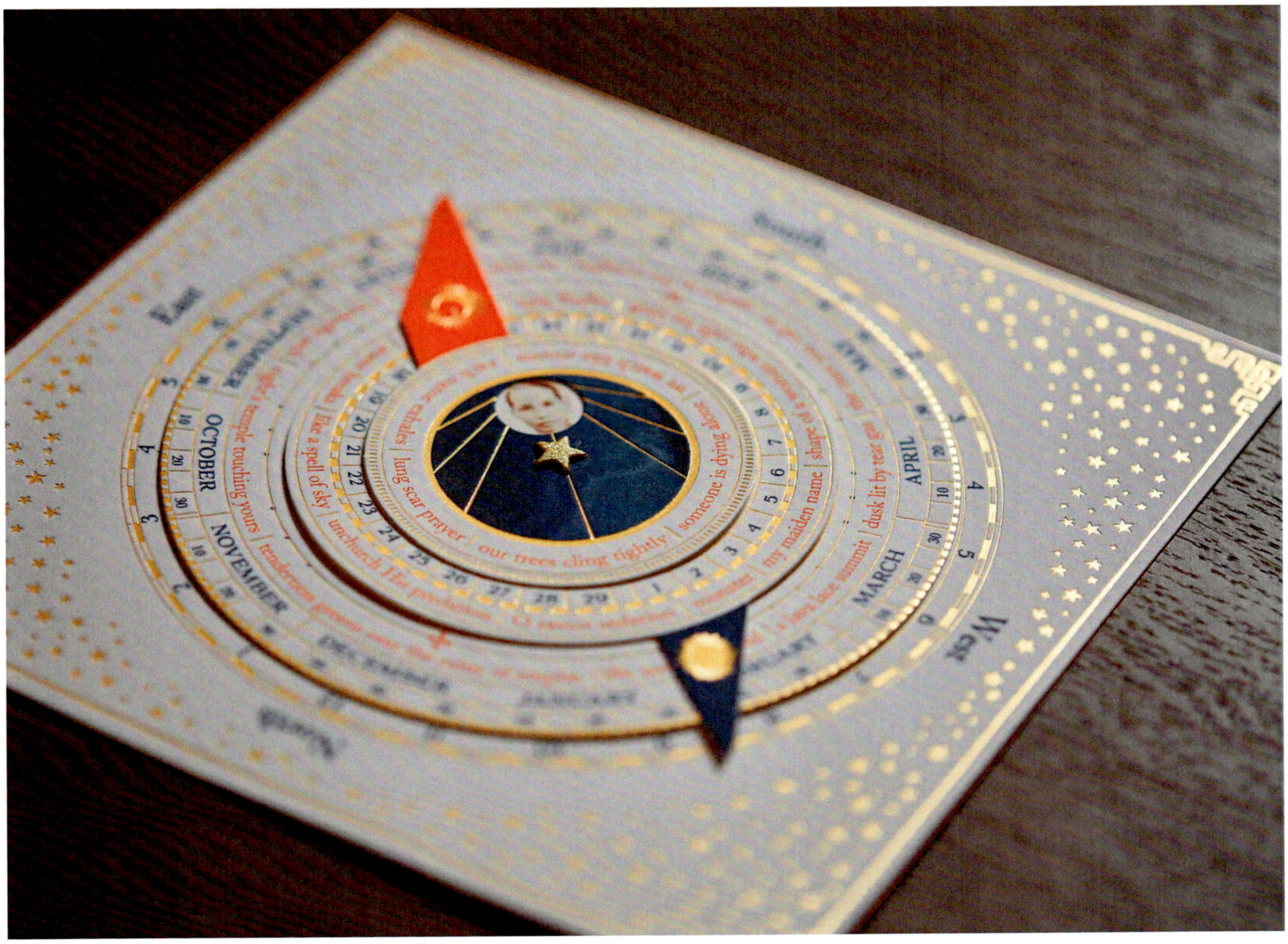

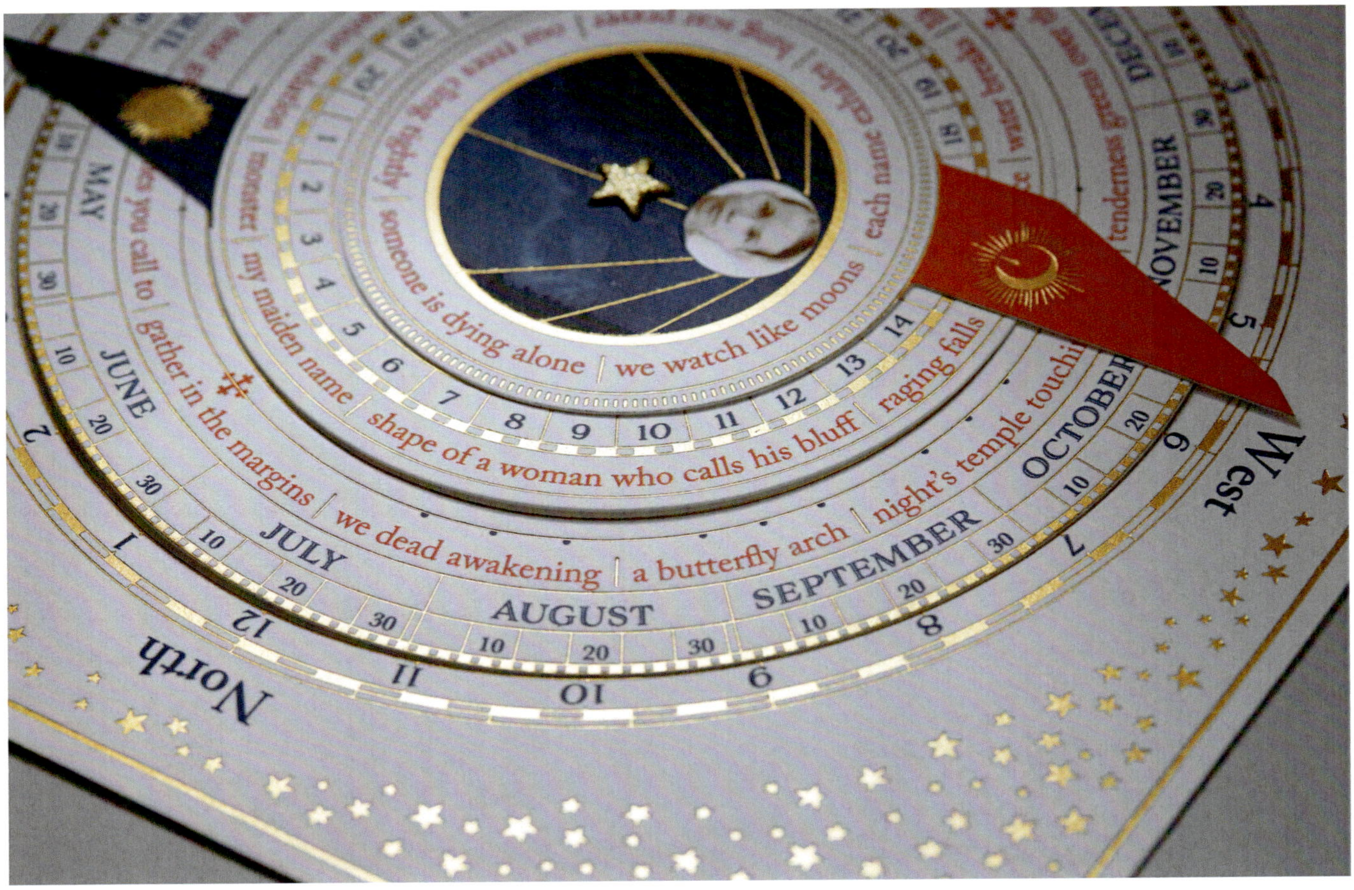

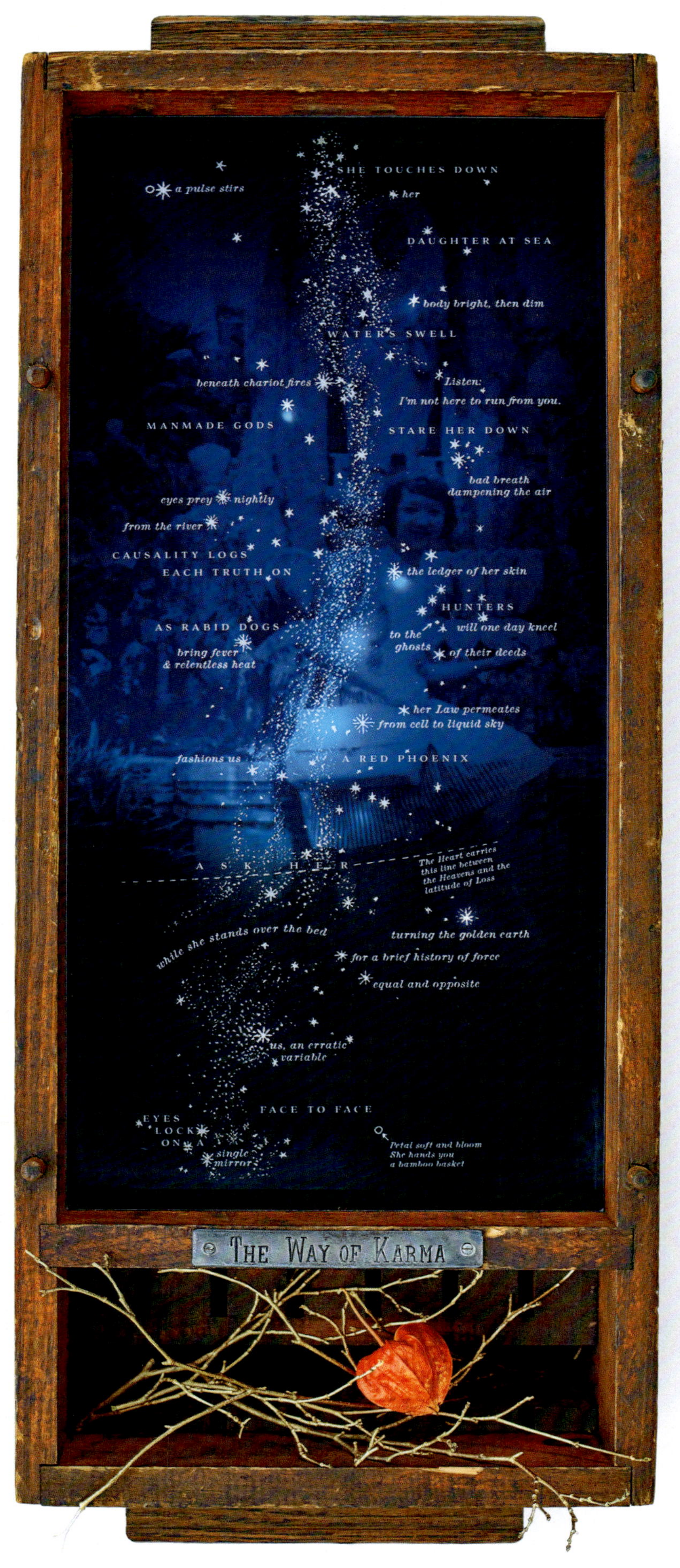

a pulse stirs
SHE TOUCHES DOWN
her
DAUGHTER AT SEA
body bright, then dim
WATERS SWELL
beneath chariot fires
Listen:
I'm not here to run from you.
MANMADE GODS
STARE HER DOWN
bad breath
dampening the air
eyes prey nightly
from the river
CAUSALITY LOGS
EACH TRUTH ON
the ledger of her skin
HUNTERS
AS RABID DOGS
to the
ghosts
will one day kneel
of their deeds
bring fever
& relentless heat
her Law permeates
from cell to liquid sky
fashions us
A RED PHOENIX
A S K H E R
The Heart carries
this line between
the Heavens and the
latitude of Loss
while she stands over the bed
turning the golden earth
for a brief history of force
equal and opposite
us, an erratic
variable
FACE TO FACE
EYES
LOCK
ON A
single
mirror
Petal soft and bloom
She hands you
a bamboo basket
THE WAY OF KARMA

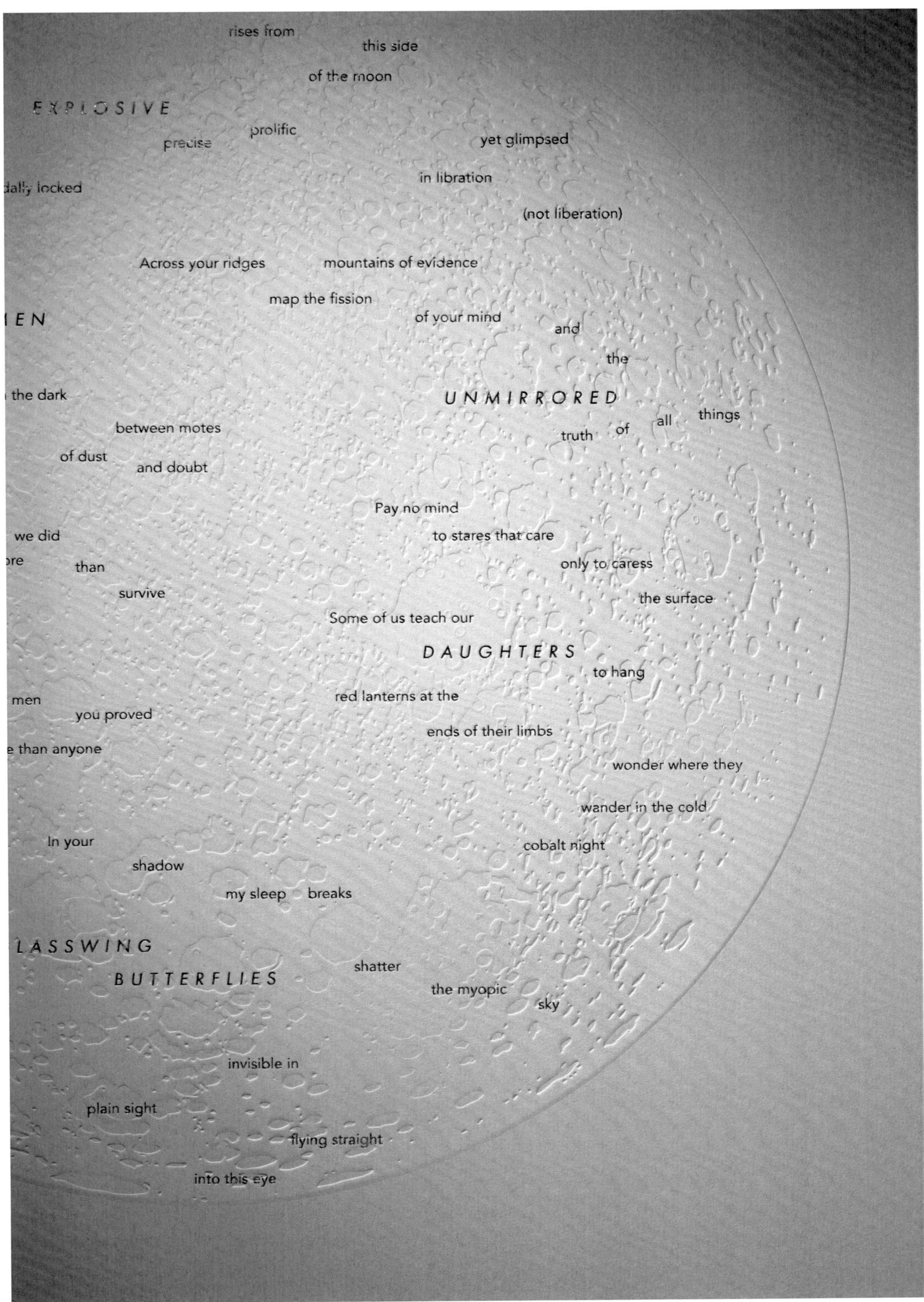
rises from
this side
of the moon
EXPLOSIVE
prolific
precise
yet glimpsed
dally locked
in libration
(not liberation)
Across your ridges
mountains of evidence
map the fission
EN
of your mind
and
the
the dark
UNMIRRORED
things
all
between motes
truth
of
of dust
and doubt
Pay no mind
we did
to stares that care
ore
than
only to caress
survive
the surface
Some of us teach our
DAUGHTERS
to hang
men
red lanterns at the
you proved
ends of their limbs
e than anyone
wonder where they
wander in the cold
In your
cobalt night
shadow
my sleep
breaks
LASSWING
BUTTERFLIES
shatter
the myopic
sky
invisible in
plain sight
flying straight
into this eye

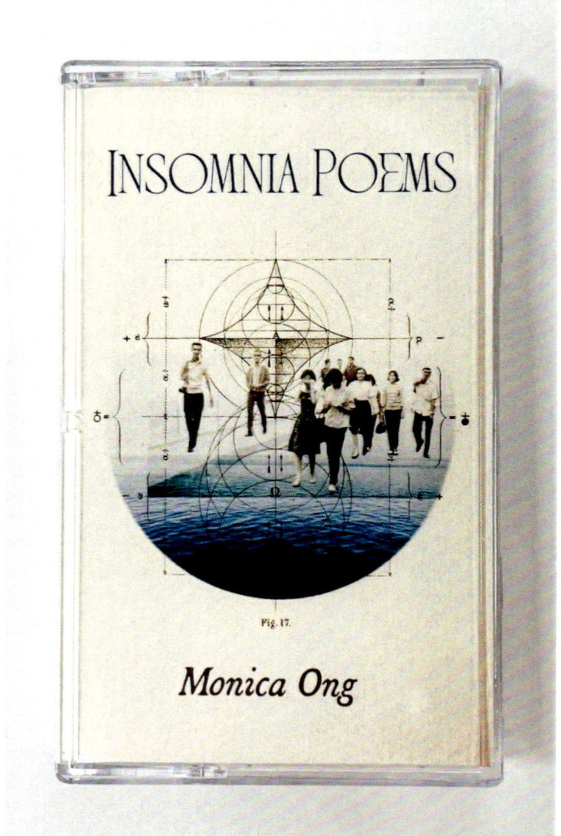
INSOMNIA POEMS
Fig. 17.
Monica Ong

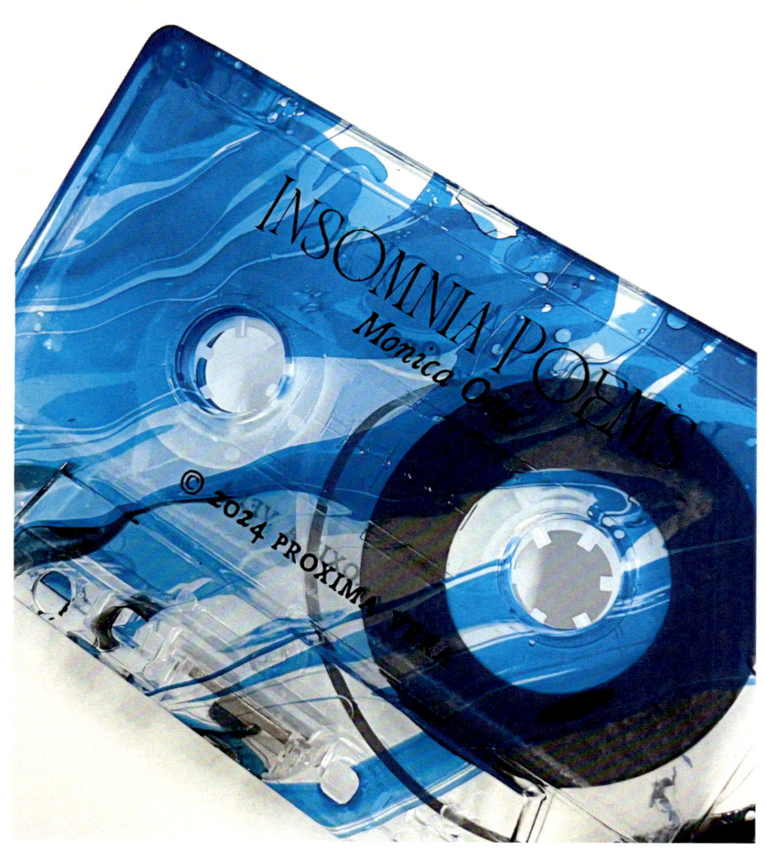
INSOMNIA POEMS
Monica Ong

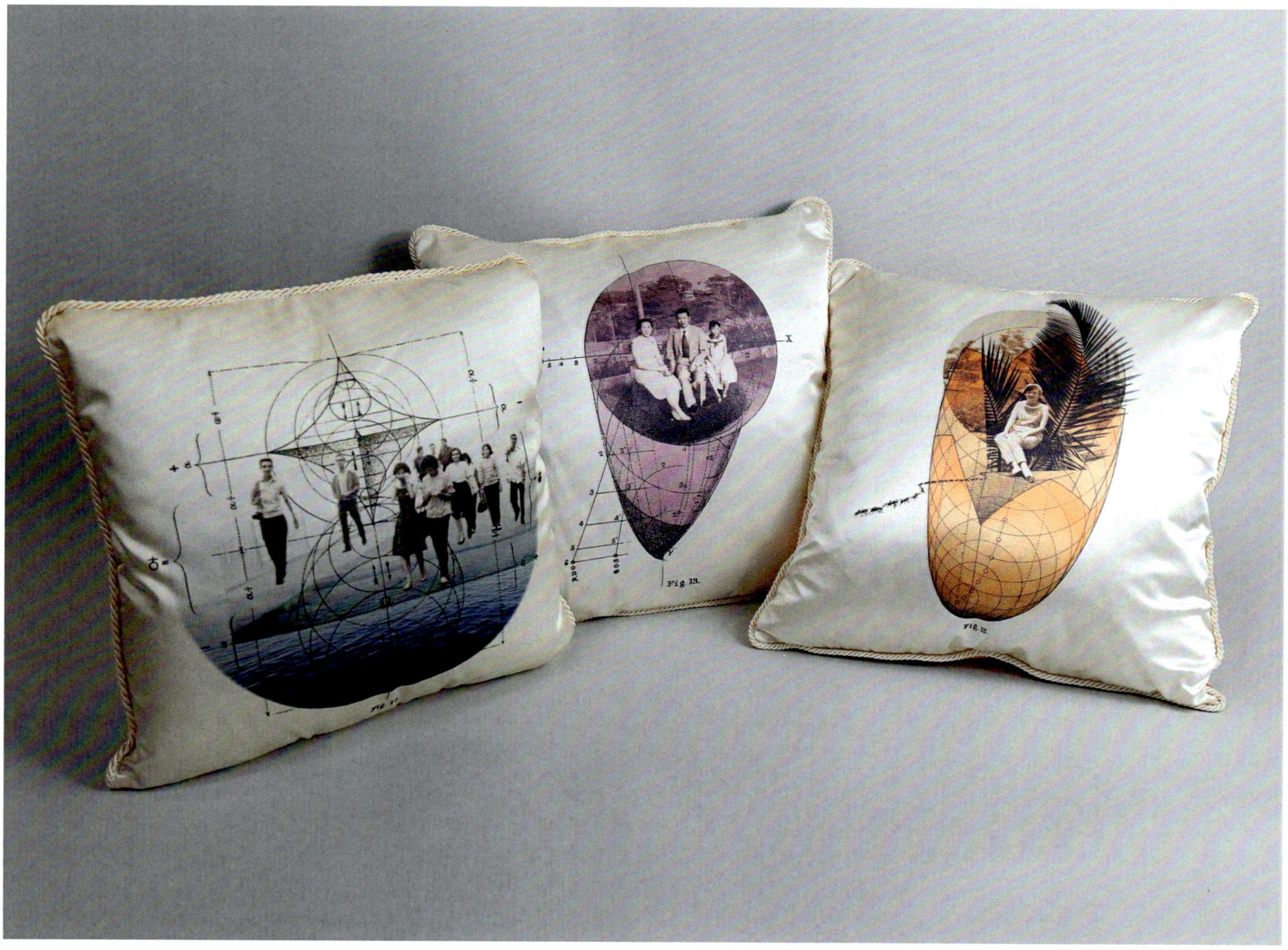

Notes and Sources

Epigraph

1. Quote is cited by Sharon Bertsch McGrayne. "Chien-Shiung Wu." *Nobel Prize Women in Science: Their Lives, Struggles, and Momentous Discoveries* (Washington, DC: Joseph Henry Press, 2002), 263.

Foreword

2. Exterior view of Chinese asterisms on building facade entryway to *Monica Ong: Planetaria* exhibition at the Poetry Foundation gallery, April 21–September 8, 2022, Chicago, Illinois.

Lavender Insomnia

3. Photo of Ong's maternal grandparents and first maternal aunt, 1957.
4. Louisa S. Cook. *Geometrical Psychology or the Science of Representation: An Abstract of the Theories and Diagrams of B. W. Betts* (London: George Redway, 1887), 119, fig. 13.

The Way of Milk

5. Photo of Ong's father with three of his siblings, c. 1949.
6. Henry W. Ruoff, editor. "The Starry Grandeur of the Milky Way." *The Circle of Knowledge: A Classified, Simplified, Visualized Book of Answers* (Boston: The Standard Publication Company, 1916), 32.

The Way of Karma

7. Photo of Ong's fourth maternal aunt, c. 1964.
8. Henry W. Ruoff, editor. "The Starry Grandeur of the Milky Way." *The Circle of Knowledge: A Classified, Simplified, Visualized Book of Answers* (Boston: The Standard Publication Company, 1916), 32.

Solstice Blessing

9. Photo of Ong's mother, c. 1964.
10. Albert A. Hopkins. "Saturn." *Our Country and its Resources* (New York: Munn & Co., Inc., 1917), 432.
11. Arthur Mee, editor. "If we could telegraph to the stars," *The Book of Knowledge: The Children's Encyclopedia, Volume 7* (New York: The Grolier Society, 1912), 1963.
12. A "kalpa" in ancient Buddhist cosmology describes an extremely long period of time that generally spans the period between the formation and disintegration of the universe.

Diaspora Nova

13. Photo of Ong's father, paternal grandparents, sister, and Ong, c. 1981.
14. Working Men's Educational Union. "Solar System," Wall hanging, c. 1860, © by National Maritime Museum, Greenwich, London. Image No. F8662.

Purple Forbidden Enclosure

15. Illustration is based on a map from Yi, Shitong, and Jacob Kistemaker. *Chinese stars and constellations in 22 maps: based on the equinox 1950: with explanatory notes.* (Amsterdam: S. N., 1986).

16. Monica Ong. *Purple Forbidden Enclosure*, 2019. Gold and silver foil stamping and letterpress print on imperial blue cover stock, 12 x 18 in. Studio collection. Production collaboration with Boxcar Press.

Amber Insomnia

17. Photo of Ong's mother, 1964.
18. Louisa S. Cook. *Geometrical Psychology or the Science of Representation: An Abstract of the Theories and Diagrams of B. W. Betts* (London: George Redway, 1887), 117, fig. 12.

White Tiger

19. Photo of Ong's fourth maternal aunt and cousin, 1975.
20. Monica Ong. *White Tiger*, 2021. Metal print, 30 x 30 in. Studio collection.

Black Tortoise

21. Alejandro Ong. Vacation photo of Tagaytay, Philippines.
22. Monica Ong. *Black Tortoise*, 2021. Metal print, 30 x 30 in. Studio collection.

Azure Dragon

23. Photo of Ong's aunties and mother, 1967.
24. Monica Ong. *Azure Dragon*, 2021. Metal print, 30 x 30 in. Studio collection.

Red Phoenix

25. Photo of Ong's father and his great uncle Yeung, c. 1952.
26. Monica Ong. *Red Phoenix*, 2021. Metal print with satin finish, 30 x 30 in. Studio collection.
27. The burning house appears in a parable in the third chapter of the Lotus Sutra, representing the threefold world and its flames, the sufferings of birth and death. The Buddha leads others out of the house towards the cart drawn by the white ox, representing the supreme teaching that buddhahood resides in all people as revealed in the Lotus Sutra. Soka Gakkai, "Parable of the three carts and the burning house," in *Dictionary of Buddhism*. Accessed May 2021. https://www.nichirenlibrary.org/en/dic/Content/P/17.

Lunar Volvelle

28. Portrait of Ong's paternal grandmother, c. 1954,
29. Monica Ong. *Lunar Volvelle*, 2021. Digital print and gold foil letterpress on natural white cover stock, 7.5 x 7.5 in. Studio collection. Production collaboration with Boxcar Press.

Indigo Insomnia

30. Photo of Ong's father with college friends, 1960.
31. Louisa S. Cook. *Geometrical Psychology or the Science of Representation: An Abstract of the Theories and Diagrams of B. W. Betts* (London: George Redway, 1887), 129, fig. 17.
32. Nichiren Daishonin quotes T'ient-t'ai in a letter written in 1274 to Ueno, the wife of Nanjō Hyōe Shichirō: "From the indigo, an even deeper blue." *Writings of Nichiren Daishonin* (Tokyo: Soka Gakkai, 1999), 456.

Syzygy

33. Agnes Giberne. *Sun, Moon, and Stars: Astronomy for beginners* (New York: American Tract Society, 1893), 135.

Her Hypothesis
34. Photo of Ong's eldest paternal uncle as a child, c. 1944.
35. Simon Newcomb. "Herschel's view of the form of the universe," *Popular Astronomy* (New York: Harper & Brothers, 1878), 477.

Who Will Give You Haircuts on Mars
36. Photo of Ong's mother, c. 1968.
37. Percival Lowell. Mars (Boston, New York: Houghton, Mifflin and company, 1895), 85.

Woman's Place in the Universe
38. Alfred R. Wallace. "Diagram of the Stellar Universe," *Man's Place in the Universe* (New York: McClure, Phillips, & co., 1903), 296.

Sanguine Insomnia
39. Parker Reed. Photo of Monica Ong, 2022.
40. Louisa S. Cook. *Geometrical Psychology or the Science of Representation: An Abstract of the Theories and Diagrams of B. W. Betts* (London: George Redway, 1887), 127, fig. 16.

Feather
41. Simon Newcomb. "Probable arrangement of the stars and nebulae visible with the telescope," *Popular Astronomy* (New York: Harper & Brothers, 1878), 477.

Sun, Not Son
42. Sir Robert Stawell Ball. "A Total Eclipse to the Girl, a Partial Eclipse to the Boy," *Star-Land* (London: Cassell & Company, Limited, 1891), 82.

Blood Moon Woman
43. Amedée Guilman. *The Heavens: An Illustrated Handbook of Popular Astronomy, edited by J. Norman Lockyer* (London: Richard Bentley, 1867), 182.
44. Li Bai. "Quiet Night Thoughts." Charles Liu (@chuckliu), translator. 2018. Twitter (now X), December 25. https://x.com/chuckliu/status/1077716492722987008.

Book of Vera
45. Epigraph and last line from Sarah Kaplan. "How Vera Rubin Changed Science," *Washington Post*, December 27, 2016, https://www.washingtonpost.com/news/speaking-of-science/wp/2016/12/27/how-vera-rubin-changed-science/.
46. Design after Byrne, Oliver. *The First Six Books of the Elements of Euclid.* (London: William Pickering, 1847), 10.

Shooting Stars
47. Ball, Sir Robert Stawell. *The Story of the Heavens.* (London: Cassell & Company, Limited, 1886. "The History of the Leonids"), 345.

Jade Insomnia
48. Photo of Ong's maternal grandmother, 1957.
49. Photo of Ong's paternal grandmother, 1941.
50. Louisa S. Cook. *Geometrical Psychology or the Science of Representation: An Abstract of the Theories and Diagrams of B. W. Betts* (London: George Redway, 1887), 107, fig. 5-6.

Her Gaze

51. Clara L. Balfour. "Caroline Herschel: Study and Work," *Women Worth Emulating* (New York: American Tract Society, 1877), 33.
52. Painted Silhouette of Caroline Herschel, c. 1770. Gunther Collection, © History of Science Museum, University of Oxford, inv. 11894.
53. Camille Flammarion. "William Herschel découvant la planete Uranus." *Astronomie populaire, description générale du ciel.* (Paris: E. Flammarion, 1890), 577.
54. Caroline Herschel discovered her first comet on August 1, 1786. Her sketches are included by her brother William Herschel in "II. Remarks on the new comet. In a letter from William Herschel, LLD. F. R. S. to Charles Blagden, M.D. Sec. R. S.," Philosophical Transactions of the Royal Society, 77:4-5. https://royalsocietypublishing.org/doi/10.1098/rstl.1787.0002
55. Monica Ong. *Her Gaze*, 2021. Custom ViewMaster reel, 4 x 4 in. Studio collection.

The Star Gazer

56. Artist rendering and translation based on T'ien-wên T'u, Hsing-chih T'ien, and Will Carl Rufus. *The Soochow Astronomical Chart* (Ann Arbor: University of Michigan Press, 1945).
57. Monica Ong. *The Star Gazer*, 2021. Letterpress gold foil stamping on natural white and navy cover stock, custom die cutting, and assembly with metal hardware, 7.5 x 7.5 in. Studio collection. Production collaboration with Boxcar Press.

Jupiter's Family of Comets

58. Photo of Ong's father in Tagaytay, Philippines, c. 1957.
59. David P. Todd. "Jupiter's Family of Comets," *A New Astronomy* (American Book Company, 1897), 401.

Yellow Insomnia

60. Photo of Ong's eldest maternal aunt, 1984.
61. Louisa S. Cook. *Geometrical Psychology or the Science of Representation: An Abstract of the Theories and Diagrams of B. W. Betts* (London: George Redway, 1887), 133, fig. 19.
62. The demon daughters are guardian deities who appear in the "Dhāranī" (twenty-sixth) chapter of the Lotus sutra and are described as protectors of those who uphold the sutra. Soka Gakkai, "Ten Demon Daughters," in *Dictionary of Buddhism*. Accessed June 2020. https://www.nichirenlibrary.org/en/dic/Content/T/44.

Daughter's Almanac

63. Frederick Alexander Black. "Diagram illustrating Effect analogues to the Aberration of Light," in *Problems in Time and Space; A Collection of Essays Relating to the Earth, Physically and Astronomically, and Cognate Matters* (London: Gall & Inglis, 1910), 123.

64. Samuel Hard Wright. *The Illustrated Family Christian Almanac for the United States* (New York: American Tract Society, 1866), 19.

65. Photo of Ong's father, c. 1960.
66. Abraham Bosse. *Traité des Pratiques Geometrales et Perspectives, Enseignées dans L'Acadmie Royale de la Peinture et Sculture* (Paris: Chez l'auteur, 1665), 97, fig. 49.
67. Anthony Joseph Gillet and William James Rolfe. *Astronomy for the Use of Schools and Academies* (New York: Potter, Ainsworth, & Co, 1882), 46, fig. 53.

68. Photo of Ong with sister and paternal grandmother, 1982.
69. Abraham Bosse. *Traité des Pratiques Geometrales et Perspectives, Enseignées dans L'Acadmie Royale de la Peinture et Sculture* (Paris: Chez l'auteur, 1665), 101, fig. 50.
70. Samuel Hard Wright. *The Illustrated Family Christian Almanac for the United States* (New York: American Tract Society, 1866), 16.
71. Anthony Joseph Gillet and William James Rolfe. *Astronomy for the Use of Schools and Academies* (New York: Potter, Ainsworth, & Co, 1882), 36, fig. 43.
72. Laurence Ilsley Hewes. *The Design of Diagrams for Engineering Formulas and the Theory of Nomography* (New York: McGraw-Hill, 1923), 81.

73. Photo of Ong's maternal grandparents, 1957.
74. Photo of Ong, c. 1981.
75. Abraham Bosse. *Traité des Pratiques Geometrales et Perspectives, Enseignées dans L'Acadmie Royale de la Peinture et Sculture* (Paris: Chez l'auteur, 1665), 116, fig. 65.
76. Laurence Ilsley Hewes. *The Design of Diagrams for Engineering Formulas and the Theory of Nomography* (New York: McGraw-Hill, 1923), 77.

77. Photo of Ong's mother, c. 1973.
78. Abraham Bosse. *Traité des Pratiques Geometrales et Perspectives, Enseignées dans L'Acadmie Royale de la Peinture et Sculture* (Paris: Chez l'auteur, 1665), 109, fig. 58.
79. Laurence Ilsley Hewes. *The Design of Diagrams for Engineering Formulas and the Theory of Nomography* (New York: McGraw-Hill, 1923), 6.

The Dark Side of the Moon

80. NASA/GSFC/Arizona State University. "Farside! And all the way around," 2009-2011, https://www.lroc.asu.edu/images/298.
81. The far side of the moon was documented by NASA's Lunar Reconnaissance Orbiter Camera with orthographic projection centered at 180° longitude, 0° latitude.
82. Monica Ong. *Dark Side of the Moon*, 2022. Embossed moon surface with text in letterpress platinum silver foil on cover stock, 16 x 22 in. Studio collection. Production collaboration with Boxcar Press.

Seagull

83. "It is I, Seagull," the first words spoken by the first woman in space, Valentina Tereshkova, during the space mission aboard Vostok 6 on June 16, 1963.
84. Type layout in the shape of NASA's Space Launch System, or SLS rocket. Composition after Joseph Cornell. *The Crystal Cage: Portrait of Berenice*, 1943.
85. Photograph of Ong's paternal cousin. 1969.
86. Maynard F. Reece. "Forney Lake," in *Waterfowl in Iowa*, by Jack W. Musgrove (Des Moines: State of Iowa, 1953), Plate XI, p. 95.

Gallery Views

87. Exterior view of *Monica Ong: Planetaria* exhibition at the Poetry Foundation gallery, April 21–September 8, 2022, Chicago, Illinois.
88. Window installations of *Diaspora Nova* and *Solstice Blessing*, Poetry Foundation.
89. Monica Ong. *The Way of Milk*, 2020. Duratrans print on acrylic, wood box, custom stamped steel, dried Chinese lantern plant, paint, LED lights. 9.5 x 22 x 4.5 in. Studio collection.

90. Additional detail views of *The Star Gazer*, 2021. Letterpress gold foil stamping on natural white and navy cover stock, custom die cutting, and assembly with metal hardware, 7.6 x 7.6 in. Studio collection.
91. Installation view of *Her Gaze* from *Planetaria* exhibition at the Institute Library, June 15–September 8, 2021, New Haven, Connecticut.
92. Interior view of *Seagull* and several Chinese constellation poems from *Monica Ong: Planetaria* exhibition at the Poetry Foundation.
93. Monica Ong. *Purple Forbidden Enclosure*, 2019. Gold and silver foil stamping and letterpress print on imperial blue cover stock, 12 x 18 in. Studio collection.
94. Detail views of *Lunar Volvelle*, 2021. Digital print and gold foil letterpress on natural white cover stock, 7.5 x 7.5 in. Studio collection.
95. Monica Ong. *The Way of Karma*, 2020. Duratrans print on acrylic, vintage wood box, custom stamped steel, dried Chinese lantern plant, paint, LED lights. 9.5 x 22 x 4.5 in. Studio collection.
96. Additional detail views of *Dark Side of the Moon*, 2022. Embossed moon surface with text in letterpress platinum silver foil on cover stock, 16 x 22 in. Studio collection. Production collaboration with Boxcar Press.
97. Monica Ong. *Insomnia Poems*, performed, designed, and edited by Monica Ong. "Yellow Insomnia" performed by Randall Horton and Monica Ong, "Sanguine Insomnia" and "Jade Insomnia" music by Boomer Harold, mastering and ink marbling by Audio Geography Studios. (Trumbull: Proxima Vera, 2024), cassette tape, 22 minutes.
98. Monica Ong. *Insomnia Pillows* based on artwork from "Indigo Insomnia," "Lavender Insomnia," and "Amber Insomnia." Custom silk pillows, 16 x 16 in. Studio collection.

Photo Documentation

Photo documentation of individual artworks by Tom Virgin, 2021–2024.
Exhibition documentation at the Institute Library of New Haven by Tom Virgin, 2021.
Exhibition documentation at the Poetry Foundation gallery by m_m<M, 2022.

Collections

Editioned works from *Planetaria* reside in the following institutional collections.

Arizona	Arizona State University – Special Collections University of Arizona Poetry Center
California	Letterform Archive – Special Collections Stanford University – Bowes Art and Architecture Library Stanford University – Special Collections University of California at Berkeley – Bancroft Library University of California at Irvine – Science Library Special Collections University of California at Santa Cruz – Special Collections
Colorado	Colorado College – Tutt Library
Connecticut	University of Connecticut at Storrs – Special Collections Wesleyan University – Special Collections and Archives Yale University – Beinecke Rare Book and Manuscript Library Yale University – Robert B. Haas Family Arts Library
Florida	University of Miami – Special Collections
Georgia	Emory University – Rose Library
Illinois	Poetry Foundation Library School of the Art Institute of Chicago University of Chicago – Special Collections University of Illinois at Urbana-Champaign – Special Collections
Indiana	Indiana University – Special Collections
Iowa	University of Iowa – Special Collections
Maine	Bowdoin College – George J. Mitchell Dept. of Special Collections
Maryland	Maryland Institute College of Art – Decker Library
Massachusetts	Amherst College – Special Collections Clark Art Institute Library – Sterling Library Smith College – Special Collections Tufts University | School of the Museum of Fine Arts – Clark Library Wellesley College – Margaret Clapp Library
Minnesota	Walker Art Center Library

Missouri	Linda Hall Library of Science, Engineering, and Technology Washington University at St. Louis – Modern Literature Collection
Nevada	University of Nevada at Reno – Special Collections
New Jersey	Princeton University – Firestone Library Special Collections
New York	Binghamton University (SUNY) – Special Collections Cornell University – Olin Library University at Buffalo Libraries (SUNY) – The Poetry Collection Vassar College – Archives and Special Collections Library
Ohio	Ohio State University – Special Collections
Pennsylvania	Franklin & Marshall College – Archives and Special Collections Haverford College – Special Collections Temple University – Charles Library, Special Collections Research Center
Rhode Island	Brown University – John Hay Library Rhode Island School of Design – Fleet Library
South Carolina	University of South Carolina – Special Collections
Tennessee	Vanderbilt University – Jean and Alexander Hearts Libraries
Texas	Baylor University – Moody Memorial Library
Utah	University of Utah – Marriott Library
Vermont	Middlebury College – Special Collections
Virginia	George Mason University James Madison University – Special Collections Rare Book School, University of Virginia – Shannon Library University of Virginia – Albert and Shirley Small Special Collections Virginia Commonwealth University – James Branch Cabell Library
Washington	University of Washington Libraries – Special Collections
Washington D.C.	Library of Congress – Rare Book and Special Collections National Museum of Women in the Arts – Library and Research Center
Wisconsin	University of Wisconsin-Madison – Kohler Art Library
Canada	McGill University Library – Special Collections University of Toronto – Special Collections
United Kingdom	History of Science Museum – University of Oxford

Acknowledgements

Many thanks to the editors and staff of the following publications in which many of the poems in this book, often in earlier version, first appeared:

Bat City Review: "Seagull"
TAB: *The Journal of Poetry & Poetics*: "Her Gaze"
Scientific American: "The Way of Karma"
Beloit Poetry Journal: "The Daughter's Almanac"
Connecticut Literary Anthology 2021: "Indigo Insomnia" (text)
POETRY Magazine: "Diaspora Nova" and "Solstice Blessing"
Dogwood: A Journal of Poetry and Prose: "Indigo Insomnia" (image)
Permafrost Magazine: "Purple Forbidden Enclosure"
A Velvet Giant: "Amber Insomnia" and "Lavender Insomnia"
Breakwater Review: "Shooting Stars"
Petrichor: A Journal of Text+Image: "Blood Moon Woman"
Tricycle: A Buddhist Review: "Yellow Insomnia"
Redivider: "Jupiter's Family of Comets"
ctrl+v: "Her Hypothesis" and "Sun, Not Son"
Waxwing Literary Journal: "Syzygy," "Woman's Place in the Universe," and "Feather"

Thank you to the following curators for including my work in their exhibitions and visions:
Alexander Campos, "Monica Ong: Celestial Bodies," Center for Book Arts
Martha Willette Lewis, "Planetaria: Visual Poetry by Monica Ong," The Institute Library
Fred Sasaki and Katherine Litwin, "Monica Ong: Planetaria," Poetry Foundation
Hildy York, "Solo Exhibition: Monica Ong," Hunterdon Art Museum
Ashara Shapiro, "Nocturne: Insomnia & Other Poems by Monica Ong," ArtWRKD
Jyothi Natarajan and Dao Strom, "De-Canon," in collaboration with Stelo Arts
Florian Carle, "Planetaria: Visual Poetry & Star Gazing," planetarium reading, Leitner Family Observatory and Planetarium, Yale Quantum Institute

I am deeply grateful to the communities at Fine Arts Work Center, Marble House Project, Martha's Vineyard Institute for Creative Writing, Millay Arts, Ragdale Foundation, the Studios at Mass MoCA, and Yaddo Foundation for fellowships that provided time, space, and nourishment to develop this collection.

The production and publication of these works would not be possible without generous support from the following programs:

Barbara Deming Memorial Fund
Connecticut Office of the Arts - Artist Fellowship Award
MassMoCA Asset for Artists Matched Savings Grant
Sustainable Arts Foundation Grant
United States Artists Fellowship

Special Thanks

Heartfelt thanks to my parents, Alejandro and Gloria, for your courage and devotion. To my siblings, Emmelyn and Chester, thank you for being my stronghold of unbreakable determination. This book is in tribute to my extended family, particularly for our elders and to all our children.

I have profound gratitude for the poets, artists, and scholars who have uplifted this endeavor with guidance and insight: Randall Horton, Victoria Chang, Brian Teare, John Yau, Adrian Matejka, Timothy Yu, Betty Bright, Marci Calabretta Cancio-Bello, Karin Roffman, Jenie Gao. Much appreciation goes to Daniel Patrick Morgan for sharing his expertise as a historian of science in ancient China. Tremendous thanks to Emily Brandt for brilliant editorial guidance and to Hyejung Kook for giving these projects such careful eyes and ears. To Beth Pickens, thank you for helping me fortify my professional foundation with sustainability and conviction.

To my dear bodhisattva family, thank you for your nourishment and compassionate wisdom. I dedicate this work to the memory of Daisaku Ikeda (1928–2023).

Thank you to Marisa Abrams, Denice Lee, Kathy Lien, Brad Larsen, Monica and Rich Chylla, Alison Perlo, Katherine Golar Morris, Frank Kensaku Saragosa, Diana Marinovic, Jacob Roesch, Boomer Harold, Ana Davis, Dave Silverman, Shirley Chock, Shanna Melton, Julie Rizzi, Adam and Mia Shopis: I can never be lost when I am near your light.

To Kay, Harry, Laura, and Maseh, thank you for filling every place you go with love. To Parker, thank you for inspiring me to make each day as kind and joyful as you. Finally, thank you Andrew, king of laughter, for your generous heart.

About the Author

Monica Ong is the author of *Silent Anatomies* (Kore Press, 2015). A graduate of the Rhode Island School of Design, Ong brings a designer's eye to experimental writing with her hybrid image-poems and installations that surface hidden narratives of women and diaspora. Her poetry can be found in *Scientific American*, *ctrl+v*, *Poetry Magazine*, and the anthology *A Mouth Holds Many Things: A De-Canon Hybrid-Literary Collection* (Fonograf Editions, 2024).

Ong's visual poetry has been exhibited nationwide including New York's Center for Book Arts, the Hunterdon Art Museum, and the Poetry Foundation. You can find her fine press visual poetry editions and literary art objects in distinguished institutional collections worldwide. In 2024, Ong was named a United States Artists Fellow.